CONTENTS

INTRODUCTION

Every gardener, even the most experienced, was once a beginner. Perhaps they had always had an interest in gardening but couldn't really do anything about it until they acquired their first garden. Or perhaps they had never given gardening a second thought until they found themselves garden owners, and were faced with the task of making the thing look respectable.

I can't turn a novice into an experienced gardener in the space of 96 pages. Nor can I make someone avowedly anti-horticultural into a prospective prize-winner. What I hope I can do, however, is to make those first steps into gardening, voluntary or otherwise, less tentative, a little less daunting and, I hope, rather exciting, enjoyable and rewarding.

There's no denying that the best of all ways to learn about gardening is to do it, and to make mistakes. Making too many mistakes can become frustrating, however, and some mistakes can be costly, so in this book, I've drawn on my own experience to give you some guidance. I've tried to avoid dogmas, however, as there are few black and whites in gardening, and few definitely

A garden can be as small as a collection of pots in a courtyard

A large vegetable garden generally comes later in your gardening life

right or definitely wrong ways of doing things. There's vast scope for personal, individual approaches and I do want to encourage you to try things and to experiment. Don't be afraid; much of gardening is simply a matter of applying common sense.

I've attempted to cover all of the aspects of gardening that you are likely to encounter in the early stages but I've excluded complex and more specialist topics that you may want to progress to later. Throughout, I've made reference to other books in my *Best* series and, as particular aspects of the subject appeal to you, I hope you will turn to these other volumes to discover more about them.

Before we begin to look at the tools you need and how you should approach your first tasks however, I want you to look at yourselves. Gardens are

extensions of our homes and lives; they should reflect a great deal about us and how we live. It's no use taking your gardening inspiration from a country estate if you have 10 square metres (12 square yards) in the middle of a city. And nor will be 'the outdoor room' concept, so beloved of garden designers, be of of use to you if you have just bought a new house surrounded by a piece of field. Every garden is different, every gardener's needs are different; and despite what folk would have you believe size is no measure of success.

Think carefully about the amount of time you have and want to devote to your garden. Think about the requirements of your family or other companions and the way that the garden should satisfy everyone's needs. Your garden will be unsuccessful, for instance, if you devote it all to vegetable growing when what your family really needs is a small

paved area with a few pots and a barbecue. It will similarly be unsuccessful if you plant pot after pot of summer flowering annuals when you will be away from home for days at a time and unable to water them. Much of gardening is about compromise: compromise between the needs of the people whose garden it is; compromise between the multifarious aspects of gardening that take up different amounts of time, effort and money; and compromise between idealised ambition and practical reality.

I have enjoyed my gardening for many summers and many winters; yet every year, almost every day that I go into the garden, I discover something that I didn't know or see something that I hadn't seen before. When you experience something similar and find it exciting, believe me, you will be hooked for life.

A growing family should make optimum use of the garden

GARDEN TOOLS

❝ *You will never be able to garden without some equipment, and the commonly repeated maxim that the more you pay, the better the product, is probably truer of garden tools than of most things. Always remember that you are not buying some disposable merchandise but are acquiring the means to enjoy your gardening for many years, if not a lifetime. But in advising you to buy the best that you can afford, I would add that gardening tools are very personal items and I strongly suggest that you never buy any that you haven't handled.* ❞

Hand tools

With hand tools, you will not be faced simply with a choice of manufacturer but also a choice between stainless steel and 'ordinary' or carbon steel.

Stainless steel is considerably more expensive but for tools with a slicing action (spades, trowels, hoes) it is my first choice. Stainless steel tools move more easily through the soil, they remain sharp for longer and they require the minimum of maintenance (wipe with a cloth after use). I advise against stainless steel forks, however, for the tines bend far too easily.

My short list of essential cultivating tools for every gardener with open garden soil to till are: a spade and fork (small border varieties rather than full-sized; these can come later if you progress to large scale vegetable growing), a hand trowel and hand fork, a push hoe and a spring-tine rake (sometimes called a lawn

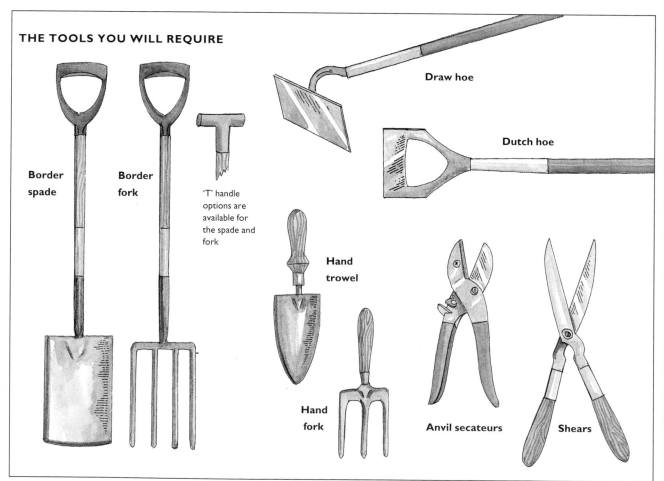

THE TOOLS YOU WILL REQUIRE

Border spade

Border fork

'T' handle options are available for the spade and fork

Draw hoe

Dutch hoe

Hand trowel

Hand fork

Anvil secateurs

Shears

...ake; this is much more versatile than
a normal garden rake with rigid teeth).
Detachable head cultivators have one
handle and several heads to enable you
to change from hoe to rake or other
long-handled appliance although I find
the inconvenience outweighs the benefits. Lightweight, aluminium handles are
better for cultivators while slightly pli-
able wood is best for spades and forks.

Cutting tools

Secateurs (and their long-handled
counterparts, loppers) are the most
important cutting tools and the choice
lies principally between scissor action
(or by-pass) models with two blades
and anvil action models with one blade.
The former deal more gently with soft
stems while the latter are valuable for
cutting hard, woody tissue without
themselves being harmed. If I could

choose only one for inexperienced
hands, it would be the anvil pattern.
Long-handled pruners and saws will
only be needed in big gardens with
large, old trees. You will need a small
pair of hand shears and, if you have a
lawn, long-handled lawn edging shears;
ideally two pairs, one to cut the top
of the lawn edge and one, with the
blades at right angles, to cut the sides.
The half-moon lawn edging knife is
relatively inexpensive but gives a
straight edge at the start of the season
in a way that no spade ever will.

Powered tools

Lawn mowers are now available in an
astonishing variety but they all work
on one of two basic principles: either
with a cylinder of rotating blades or
with some form of whirling slasher,
which these days is more likely to be
of nylon than metal. My preferences lie
with the large petrol-engined wheeled
rotary, the petrol-engined cylinder and
electric cylinder (all with grass collectors) and the small electric hover
rotary. If I had one small lawn, I would
use the electric cylinder. As it is, I have
fairly large lawns of fairly good turf, so
have all of the remaining three, using
the big rotary mower (which is really
at home on rougher, tougher grass),
early in the season while the surface is
slightly uneven, wet and still littered
with the debris of winter, the big cylinder mower during the summer to give
a smooth finish and attractive stripes
and the small hover to reach beneath
overhanging shrubs and into difficult
corners. I hope this will indicate the
type you will find the most useful for
particular gardens.

After a powered lawnmower, powered hedge trimmers would be my next
labour-saving purchase but while I have
suggested a lawn rake as your only garden rake, it will be of little use for the
periodic removal of moss from a lawn
of any reasonable size and it is here
that powered lawn rakes are invaluable.
Their collectors, however, are uselessly
small and much the best plan is to use
the machine without the collector and
to rake the moss and 'thatch' into
heaps afterwards.

The only remaining power tool that I
now place among my gardening indis-
pensables is a compost shredder, but
bear in mind that while the debris from
a small garden can be coped with by a
small electric shredder of around 1000
watts, larger gardens really need large
electric or, better still, petrol-engined
machines, which are very expensive.

**Electric hedge trimmers are an
important powered tool**

**A compost shredder has become
invaluable in this recycling age**

YOUR GARDEN SOIL

There is no more precious asset in your garden then the soil. It must be cared for and respected. It is easier, of course, for someone with a fine rich loam to believe this than it is for a gardener with a light, free-draining sand or, worse still, a soil so heavy that a dinner plate could be fashioned from it. But it is as true nonetheless as my next statement: every soil can be improved and every soil is potentially fertile.

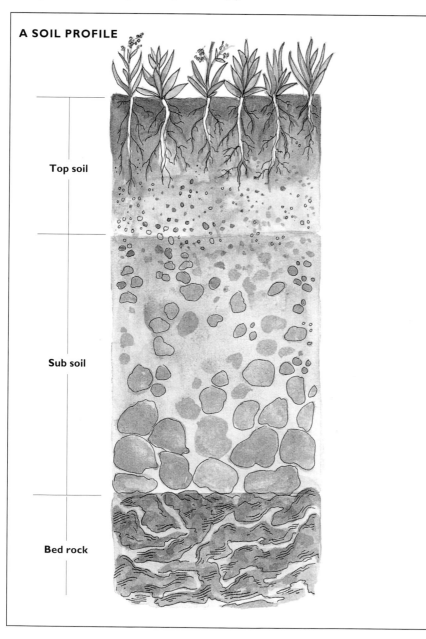

A SOIL PROFILE

Top soil

Sub soil

Bed rock

The soil is not only important but also very complex, although a basic understanding of what it is and what it does is all that is needed to ensure that your gardening activities are productive. I shall introduce you, therefore, to two of the most important characteristics of soil: its texture and its structure. A soil's texture is determined by the relative amounts it comprises of three types of mineral particles. In decreasing size, these are sand, silt and clay. It's quite easy to see these components by shaking up a small sample of soil with water in a bottle and then allowing the sediment to settle. The dense sand settles first at the bottom, the less dense silt next and the clay (often after a long time) on top. Rubbed between moistened fingers, a very sandy soil feels gritty, a very clayey soil feels greasy.

A clay soil is hard to cultivate, poorly draining and very slow to warm up in spring, but the minute clay particles do hold plant nutrients very effectively. A sandy soil, by contrast, is easy to dig, quick to warm up but drains freely, losing both water and nutrient as it does so. The ideal soil for most gardening activities is a loam, a general term for a soil that contains a readily workable blend of sand, silt and clay. You can't alter the natural proportions of the three types of mineral matter in your soil but you can alter the structure of the soil. A soil's structure is determined by the balance of mineral and other matter, water and air, and it affects how well the soil forms into crumbs. The key to improving the structure is organic matter or humus: the dead remains of plants partially decomposed through the activity of soil fungi and bacteria.

Soil type dictates much of what you can grow; only an acid soil will support rhododendrons

Humus has sponge-like properties that improve the moisture retentiveness of a sandy soil, yet it also contains natural glues that help to bind the mineral matter into crumbs, between which are spaces. This process operates in sandy soils and heavy clays too so, paradoxically, the same material can improve both free-draining and waterlogged soils. If you regularly add organic matter to your soil, your gardening will inevitably improve. If the garden is large, then do a little thoroughly at a time, rather than spreading both organic matter and effort too thinly.

The soil in any garden plot or bed should be dug when plants are removed from it and this is the time when organic matter is most easily incorporated. With a normal vegetable plot or annual flower bed, this will generally be every year, in the autumn. With a deep vegetable bed, (see page 24), it will be every five or six years. With a herbaceous border or soft fruit garden, it might be every seven or 10 years.

With a shrubbery, it could be only twice in a gardening life, although the soil must be dug locally whenever an individual tree or shrub is removed. The reason for digging is to correct the accumulated structural damage: a vegetable plot will have been walked on, the soil compressed and the crumb structure and drainage impaired. Even if you rarely walk through your ornamental beds and borders, the natural beating activity of rain will effectively compress the soil over time.

YOUR GARDEN SOIL

SINGLE DIGGING

Dig out a single trench and remove the soil to the end of the plot you are digging. This trench is then filled with the soil turned over to create the second trench and so on to the end of the plot. Work in some well rotted manure or compost as you do this. The final trench is filled by the soil removed from the first trench

Single digging. At its simplest, digging entails turning over the soil with a spade or fork, preferably in a systematic fashion from one side of the plot to the other. If it is done in autumn, the clods can be left fairly large because the action of winter rain and frost will break them down further. As the soil is turned, so organic matter in the form of compost or manure can be roughly forked in. The activity of worms during the winter will ensure that it is dragged down and more thoroughly mixed into the soil. This type of digging, called single-digging, is generally satisfactory for a plot that is dug annually but the accumulated effects of several years without cultivation necessitate a more thorough operation. This is called double digging and it is hard but valuable work.

Double digging To double dig, you should work from side to side of the area as before but the soil should be removed to two spades depth; in effect to produce a trench about 45cm (1½ft) deep each time you cross the plot. Organic matter should be laid in the bottom of trench and forked in thoroughly. Then more organic matter should be forked in as the trench is filled with soil from the adjoining trench.

After texture and structure, the third important soil feature of which you should be aware is its relative acidity or alkalinity, for this, in part, dictates how well your plants will grow. Unlike texture and structure, however, acidity and alkalinity can be quantified relatively easily, using a scale called pH. The lower the pH, the more acidic the soil. The pH of soils in Britain ranges from

DOUBLE DIGGING

Step 1
Remove soil from the first trench and take to end of the plot, ready to fill the final trench dug

Soil from first trench, to fill final trench

Step 2
Dig over the exposed layer of the first and subsequent trenches with a fork. Work in some well rotted manure or compost as you do this

Manure or well rotted compost

|— 45 cm (1½ ft) —|

about 3 for a very acidic peat to about .5 for a very thin soil overlying chalk. The full chemical pH scale spans from ? to 14 and the mid-point, 7, is called neutral). Most types of plant have difficulty in taking up essential mineral nutrients from an alkaline soil because they become combined together chemically. On page 8, I suggest some ways of ensuring that plants can receive their required nutrients under these conditions, but for most types of plant (and certainly for most fruit and vegetables), a soil that is slightly acidic (with a pH of about 6.5) will give the best results.

How can you discover how close your soil is to this ideal, and what can be done to alter it? Quite the easiest way of roughly gauging the pH of your soil is to look at the vegetation growing naturally or in neighbouring gardens in your area. If there are rhododendrons

and azaleas nearby, your soil will be acidic. If raspberries have yellow leaves with dark green veins, it will be alkaline. Much the best way to test your soil pH more precisely is with a testing kit that depends on using a coloured dye; I don't find so-called pH meters very accurate. If, after testing your soil, you want to adjust the pH, you can do so, but only within limits. To reduce the acidity, you must use garden lime, best applied in the autumn. Because the amount to add will depend both on the type of soil and its initial pH, most lime manufacturers supply a graph or chart to show how much lime to add. Check the pH again after application to see if a further addition is needed but never add lime to soil as a matter of routine. If your soil is naturally alkaline, there is much less that you can do to change it, although adding proprietary sulphur

chips will give a small increase in acidity on a localised scale.

One further aspect of soil management that is most important with vegetable growing is the concept of rotation: a device to ensure that the same type of crop isn't grown on the same area more than once every three years. The reason is two-fold: different plants require different types of nutrient and so the whole range of soil nutrients will be utilised; and pests and diseases, specific to different types of crop, will die away in their absence, although this is only really true for very large cultivated areas. Nonetheless, rotation is a good basis for vegetable gardening and on page 58, at the beginning of the Vegetable section of the book, I have included a basic scheme.

Step 3
As you dig out the area of the second and subsequent trenches place the soil on top of the area dug over with the fork in Step 2

Manure or well rotted compost

Manure or well rotted compost

Soil from first trench

Step 4
The final trench of your plot is filled with the soil removed from the very first trench you dug out in Step 1

PLANNING YOUR GARDEN

It's an inescapable fact that most gardens appear as they do more by accident than design. There are two main reasons for this. First, a gardener taking over an established garden is generally reluctant to change the existing layout, or at least to change it very quickly or extensively. This may be because of lack of time, lack of inclination, or simply because it is difficult to grasp how significantly a garden could be improved by relatively small but well thought out design changes. Second, on a new site, financial limitations or a belief that the task is just too big may prevent new gardeners from planning their garden in its entirety. They are content to let things evolve piecemeal. I hope, nonetheless, that I can persuade you that planning your garden is really a matter of applied common sense.

I find it useful to approach garden design through three basic questions:

1. What does your garden site offer you?
2. How can your garden function effectively for you?
3. How do you make your garden appear larger than it really is?

In a small area, it's sensible to mix ornamentals and edible crops

A lawn is ideal for keeping the centre of your garden open and uncluttered

PLANNING YOUR GARDEN

What does your garden site offer you?

Your soil will dictate to a greater or lesser extent the types of plant that you can grow; to a greater extent if it is markedly acidic or alkaline; to a lesser extent if it is merely very sandy or clayey. I doubt, however, that there are any garden features that would be totally out of the question in particular soils, provided you are prepared to compromise slightly on the choice of plants.

The topography of the site (the humps, hollows and slopes) certainly influences the ease with which digging or lawn mowing can be performed, but it can affect your design in a positive way too. A slope is always the best position for a rock garden; the top of a slope is the best place in a generally sloping garden for a fairly formal pool, while the foot of a slope is best for an

informal one where the margins are to be softened with bog and waterside plants because of the natural overflow of water at the edges. The base of a hollow or even the foot of a slope is often a poor place for a fruit garden because dense, cold, frosty air accumulates there and will damage the blossom. And this type of position is also no place for slightly tender or early leafing or blossoming ornamentals. Conversely, the top of a slope is often a windy place and this too will make for an unproductive fruit garden because pollinating insects are blown away.

The only existing plants that are truly important in influencing a garden design are trees because, even with modern technology and great deal of money, planting really big trees is a fantasy for most of us. Many very good gardens are

largely designed around one or more mature trees for these generally dictate where much of the light and shadow lies and, because they draw heavily on the food and water reserves of the soil also dictate where you can't position vegetable and fruit gardens or mixed borders. The presence of trees, especially deciduous trees will also influence the positioning of the pools and the greenhouse, neither of which benefit from shade or falling leaves. But does your garden also have special and unusual natural features? Among those that I consider valuable and important enough to justify reorganising other garden activities are a natural outcrop of rock that offers you the chance to have a real rock garden; and a stream or even a wet ditch around which you can plant a bog garden.

How can your garden function effectively for you?

Try to position features thoughtfully. A vegetable garden must have as much sun as possible, yet as it isn't always the most attractive feature, it may be necessary to screen it from the rest of the garden without the screen itself casting much shade. Positioning the vegetable plot on the sunnier and more sheltered boundaries of the garden is the easiest way to do this. The alternative approach of course, is to make your vegetable garden more attractive by interspersing the vegetables with flowers, and by arranging the vegetables carefully in an aesthetically pleasing way. A herb garden is almost always both functional and attractive, both

ends being served by having it as close as possible to the kitchen. When positioning purely ornamental beds and borders, be sure to place them where they can be appreciated at the time of year they will be at their best. This is most important in relation to a shrubbery grown for winter colour; there's little point in placing it at the furthest point from the house where no-one is likely to go in winter.

The second way in which your garden can be made to function well is to ensure that it is designed for labour-saving maintenance. As you begin to garden, you will soon discover the ways in which some features are much more

labour-intensive than others but I can best illustrate the point in relation to design with two common examples. One of the most time-consuming gardening tasks is in trying to mow twists and corners of a lawn that are too small for the mower and are therefore either left untidy or must be cut laboriously with shears. The other example is that of a gravel path adjoining a lawn, which is visually lovely, but you must be prepared for occasionally having to brush stones from the grass while a gravel path adjoining a vegetable plot can be a nightmare as you walk from soil to gravel and pick up vast quantities of the path on your muddy footwear.

In a small courtyard garden, a lawn is both inappropriate and impractical

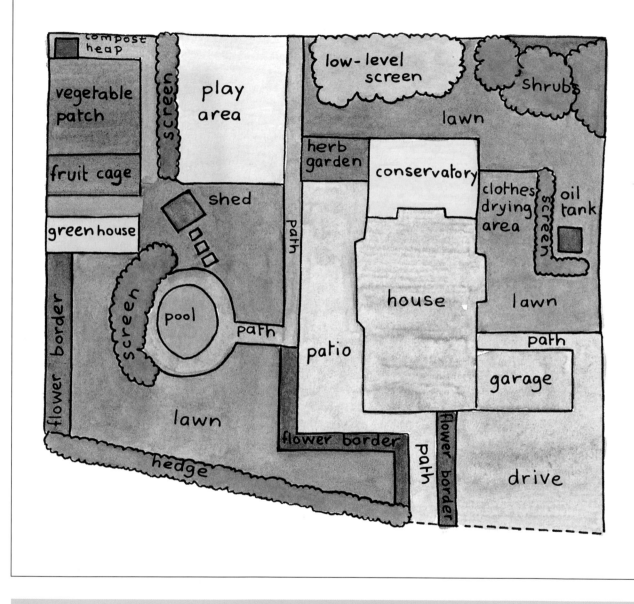

How do you make your garden appear larger than it really is?

Creating an illusion of space is not difficult in most gardens; and very rewarding too. Give the impression that there are a great many plants in your garden while at the same time filling relatively little of the area with them. The simplest way to achieve this apparent conjuring trick is to keep the centre of the garden open (with a lawn is the easiest way) and confine most of your plants to the periphery. This also has the advantage of obscuring the boundary fence or wall, so making it impossible to see where your property ends. This effect can be improved still further if there is pen space beyond your garden (fields r parkland for instance) that can be limpsed through gaps in these marginal lantings. But do take care not to make our boundary so tall that neighbouring ardens will suffer in consequence. Make good use of curves in lawns, beds, orders and paths to suggest that there s something beyond what can actually e seen. Placing a focal point so that it s glimpsed through an archway or a ap between two plantings also helps o take the eye a long way and enhance he feeling of distance.

Having decided, I hope, that your arden would benefit from a degree of lesign or re-design, you will need to know how many of the changes must be worked out in detail beforehand. I have a suspicion that many would-be designers of their own gardens are put off by the detailed scale plans (often beautifully executed in water-colours) that they may have seen in books and magazines. These might be fine for professionals and theorists but I have never seen such a plan translated into practice without considerable modification. I find it much more effective simply to equip yourself with several sheets of plain paper on which the outline of your garden is shown, place yourself at advantage point (usually a bedroom window) and start to sketch in the various features that you want to retain or introduce. The most important single feature is a focal point but the precise positioning of this can only be decided from ground level when you look at the garden from the various possible viewpoints: windows, house doorways, gates or paths. In a large garden, you will very probably require more than one focal point to provide visual satisfaction from different spots. It really does all boil down eventually to common sense.

Try not to obscure any green areas beyond your garden; the view will make your garden seem bigger

THE FABRIC OF YOUR GARDEN

❝ Although gardeners think automatically of plants and planting when planning a garden, there is a rather more to it than that. In reality, I'm not at all sure that the non-living framework isn't the more important indicator of mood, style and purpose. So you should take at least as much care in your choice of the 'hard' parts of your garden as in your choice of plants; and remember that mistakes made there will be very much more difficult to rectify; transplanting a paved courtyard is no easy matter. ❞

Paths and terraces

Paths provide the means to move easily from one part of the garden to another, not only for people but also for wheelbarrows or lawnmowers. Their width and the sharpness of any corners must take account of this and a path less than about 65cm (2¼ft) wide will create problems; paths to accommodate wheelchairs, of course, must be wider. Terraces, courtyards or patios are generally for sitting out on and they must be large enough to accommodate garden furniture. They should also be placed where they will catch the most sun but also be sheltered and private.

Constructional materials

Bark in ornamental grades is excellent for laying beneath climbing frames or swings and for forming rustic paths through planted parts of the garden. For paths, bark should be laid approximately 4–5cm (1½–2in) deep.

Bricks must be able to withstand the wear and tear of being walked on and be frost tolerant. Modern 'engineering' bricks are suitable as are bricks specially made for the purpose and sometimes called paviours. They may be laid in a great variety of patterns, the particular pattern chosen dictating the overall feel of the area.

Concrete is relatively inexpensive but should not be used for continuous areas of more than about 3 square metres (3 square yards) because of problems with its expansion and contraction. It is also visually dull and can be slippery when wet. Frankly, I can find no good use for it in the garden other than for greenhouse or shed foundations.

Gravel (either real gravel, comprising small naturally rounded particles or an artificial gravel in the form of crushed stone) is not only the cheapest material with which to cover a large area, I believe it is also one of the best. Gravel almost flows into difficult corners and around irregular shapes, looks attractive in combination with almost all other materials and is very easy to plant into. But don't use it where muddy boots will trample across it.

Pebbles and cobbles laid very carefully and set in mortar can be used to create a path but will always be difficult to walk on, and even harder to push wheeled vehicles over.

Pre-cast and natural slabs of reconstituted or artificial stone are excellent. Occasionally, you may be able to obtain second-hand slabs of real stone but otherwise, I advise you to choose the artificial alternative which is much easier to lay, being of uniform thickness.

Sets (or setts) are brick-like blocks of natural stone, often granite, or artificial replicas. They can be extremely attractive when used in small quantities and arranged in some geometric pattern, especially in combination with other paving materials.

Tarmac is a splendid invention for roads and pavements but use it in your garden and it too will look like roads and pavements.

Wood is often suggested as suitable for paths or larger areas. It isn't. If smooth, it is dangerously slippery when wet, a problem enhanced as it ages; if rough, it will have dangerous splinters.

Vary the type of paving you use to add interest and attractiveness

Areas for sitting out should be close to the house to be practical

Garden boundaries can be made more appealing than a simple fence

Boundaries

I believe that, in almost all situations, there is no better boundary for a garden than a hedge and on page 46, I discuss their merits. But there are some gardens where a hedge would be too expensive, would look inappropriate or would be too slow growing. The other possibilities are a wall or a fence.

In some areas dry stone or other types of wall have become integral parts of the landscape and should be used if possible. In many old town gardens, brick walls too are important features of the urban landscape and, whenever possible, should be repaired rather than replaced with fencing. But in modern gardens, modern materials are appropriate and a large range of

attractive building blocks is now available, many with gaps as part of their integral design.

The most popular modern fence is built from panels of some form of overlapping softwood planks. But it is the most popular because it is the cheapest. It lacks both wind permeability and physical strength and where it must be the choice, ensure that every vertical post is braced by a diagonal. The drab effect can be relieved by having the posts 30cm (1ft) taller than the fence and erecting trellis along the top. This will enable you to train roses, clematis or other climbers most attractively though it will reduce structural stability. A good alternative and only a little more costly than softwood panels and much prettier, are hurdles; the best and most durable, I find, are of willow.

CREATING PLANTING AREAS

Choosing the most appropriate places to grow your ornamental plants, and then fitting the different types of planting areas together will greatly enhance the pleasure that you and others will derive from looking at your garden. This sounds simple, but isn't as straightforward as you might wish or imagine because almost every type of plant can be displayed in different ways. I shall indicate the main possibilities, but remember that experimentation and personal individuality are what make gardens so fascinating. My suggestions are intended as a starting point for your own ideas.

Beds and borders

There is no hard and fast division between what constitutes a bed and a border, although a bed is very commonly taken to mean a planting of annuals or other temporary plants whereas a border is a more long-term planting. Whatever you call it, a planting of short-term plants will, by definition, require regular work and cost in replanting if it is to give year-round interest. If you want something more long term and much less labour-intensive, then you should choose a shrubbery (below). If you are prepared for some regular work but little re-planting then a herbaceous border of perennials or a mixed border of herbaceous perennials amongst a permanent framework of shrubs will provide the answer. In any permanent planting, however, remember that gaps may be filled at any time with annuals, bulbs or, very effectively, with ready-planted containers.

By implication, a border generally borders something: a lawn, a wall or other boundary for example. There is however a type of planting that doesn't. It is called an island bed; it sits, like an island, in a lawn and it may be planted either with annuals or with perennials. Many gardens have them and many gardeners enjoy them; I don't. Unless an island bed is big enough and contains plants that are tall enough for you not to be able to see around it, I think it looks frankly ridiculous and can diminish the impact of a beautiful lawn.

Shrubberies

A shrubbery is simply a bed or border devoted to shrubs; although generally better with a few, low growing perennials and bulbs interplanted. The shrubs may be evergreen or deciduous (a mixture of the two will ensure year-round interest) and a range of varieties can be chosen with foliage, blossom and/or ornamental fruiting appeal. In a large shrubbery, it is usual to include one or two small trees to give additional height although a wide range of heights is available among the shrubs themselves. A shrubbery is generally very easy to maintain, one or two applications of fertiliser and a small amount of annual renewal pruning (see page 86 and *Best Pruning*) being all that is usually required and it is a very important and attractive component of gardens both large and

Herbaceous borders are best as a garden boundary but are labour intensive

Island beds in lawns are now becoming old-fashioned

range of 'background' colours to complement your plants, and it still has sufficient novelty appeal to be interesting in its own right. Allied to gravel gardens are pebble beds, where the plants are placed among pebbles and, perhaps loveliest of all, although not easy to do, stream-bed gardens which mimic the appearance of stony stream beds during the dry seasons of Australia, South Africa and other places.

Acid soil beds

There is a temptation, and one that I have succumbed to, for gardeners with neutral or alkaline soil to want to grow rhododendrons, camellias and other plants that require acidic conditions. Provided your ambitions are kept within limits and you choose small or dwarf varieties, it is perfectly possible. Using containers with ericaceous compost is one possibility, but creating a small acidic soil bed, confined with

small. Most rose plantings in gardens are simply shrubberies dedicated to roses although, as I indicate on page 38, I don't necessarily think this is the best way to grow them.

Containers

I discuss container gardening on page 54 but remember that any plants can be grown in a container and containers may be positioned anywhere in the garden. They can, if you wish, form your entire ornamental plantings, something that is done in many small town gardens.

Gravel and similar gardens

A gravel garden is a planting in which the surface of the soil is covered with gravel. It can be a bed or border in its own right or simply a planted area at the edge of a gravelled walkway. Such

a planting has many virtues: weed control is aided by the presence of the gravel which also acts as a moisture-maintaining mulch, it is possible to walk among the plants in a way that can't be done with bare soil, it offers a wide

Alpines are best grown in raised beds rather than old-style 'rockeries'

planks, logs, stones or in some similar manner is another. At one time, I would have advocated filling this with a mixture of peat and soil, but peat is now recognised as a precious resource, to be used in gardening only in small amounts and when there is absolutely no alternative. There are a number of acidic composts now available, based on bark and other materials and while not as effective as peat, they will fulfil the same role in an acidic soil bed tolerably well.

Paving plantings

Paving slabs, bricks, stone sets and similar materials (see page 18) are now to be found in most gardens; and in most cases they have plants growing in the cracks between them. But unfortunately, the plants concerned tend to be weeds. This is a shame for a wonderful

A shrubbery is the easiest of all types of planting to manage

effect is being lost and a wonderful planting opportunity being neglected by not deliberately introducing ornamental plants. You must, of course, select plants that are tolerant of being trodden on and you are most likely to find an appropriate selection in the rock garden/alpine section of your nursery or garden centre.

Grassy areas

In most gardens, a grassy area is a lawn and, therefore, it is a place for mown grass (page 48). If the idea of having drifts of bulbs or native flowers growing through grass in your garden appeals to you, please don't confuse such a place with a lawn. While a few small bulbous plants, such as crocuses or aconites, might be appropriate at the edges of a large lawn or around old and well established trees, anything more ambitious than this will look a mess. Mixtures of grass with other plants must allow for the grass being left unmown for long periods and are really only appropriate for larger, wilder areas and in orchards, where they can look wonderful.

Rock gardens

A rock garden is one, albeit the most obvious, way of growing alpine plants. It isn't the only option, however, and some form of container (either a trough or a raised bed page 55) is probably an easier solution in a small garden. An alpine greenhouse will be the choice of gardeners wanting to build up an extensive collection, particularly of the more challenging kinds. If a rock garden is what you want, look

at the way that rock gardens are constructed in botanic gardens or similar places to see how they are formed. They aren't simply piles of soil with stones on the top. The whole area has to be dug over and grit or other material introduced to improve drainage, the stone should be of a type appropriate to your locality, the individual rocks must be arranged very carefully in a manner that imitates natural rock formations, and they must be obtained from an approved quarry source.

Isolated specimens

Almost any plant can be grown as an isolated specimen but, clearly, the effect will be minimal if it isn't of significant size. Trees, large shrubs and large grasses or other herbaceous perennials (especially evergreen types) are the obvious choices and they can be used

Mixed borders have largely replaced herbaceous plantings

o form the focal points that I described earlier (page 17). Be sure to prepare planting positions thoroughly and, if the plant is to be placed in a lawn or other grassed area, be sure to allow an area of up to 1m (3ft) in diameter of bare soil around the base to avoid competition for water and nutrients.

Woodland

A woodland in a garden is, more strictly, likely to be a copse but if you have a garden of say, 0.5 hectares (1.25 acres) or more, then a small group of trees can be a most attractive feature in its own right and also will give you the opportunity to grow a range of shade-loving woodland plants beneath. But do make your tree selection carefully and be sure that you aren't choosing species that are so vigorous and tall that they will, in a few years time, be on their way to creating a small forest.

Wet areas

Plants grow naturally in all manner of habitats and those that grow in wet places are among the prettiest and most appealing. If they are truly aquatic types, then the garden pool (page 50) is the place for them but if they simply require permanently wet soil, then a bog garden is what is needed. If you have an area that naturally has impeded drainage and remains permanently wet, then you should take advantage of it. If you don't, then you can create one using a plastic pond liner but fill it with wet soil instead of water. Do remember however that you will need to top it up with water in dry weather and this can be a tedious task.

A gravel garden looks striking and is easy to maintain

BUYING PLANTS

" Among the greatest pleasures of gardening is that you can add, year by year, to your range of plants. You can do this of course by buying packeted seed (or even by saving your own), and sowing it either indoors or out, as I describe on page 26. But beginning with a plant rather than seed will give you a head start and buying plants from garden centres or nurseries rather than raising your own offers you big advantages; provided you know what to look for and how to look for it. "

Annual bedding plants and vegetables

Here you will have been spared the time, trouble and expense involved in sowing, germinating and pricking-on a large number of plants. You may not, however, have been spared the task of hardening off (page 26) for trays of young plants are too often taken straight from the propagating house to the display area without being properly accustomed to the outdoors. I still see far too many outlets offering half-hardy plants for sale long before the likely date of the last frost. Unless you have a greenhouse, cold frame or comparable

holding area, you will soon be returning for replacements.

Buying annual plants, rather than raising them yourself, means that you will pay proportionately very much more to

off-set the nursery's own costs and provide them with a profit. But on balance, unless you are very enthusiastic and have a great deal of time to spare, I'm sure that buying common bedding makes a good deal of sense for many gardeners. For those plants required in small numbers and for uncommon types that are less likely to be stocked at garden centres, raising them from seeds represents a better, if not the only option.

The situation with vegetables is rather different for most are sown directly outdoors. And in general

Bare-rooted plants sent by mail

A huge range of bedding plants is now obtainable from garden centres

hose few types that are better raised for transplanting (sweet corn for instance) are required in small numbers that should be within most gardeners' production capabilities; they tend to be fairly quick growing and in consequence, can be sown later so that the artificial heat required is unlikely to be prohibitively expensive. A major exception is the brassicas: cabbages, cauliflowers, Brussels sprouts and their kin which can be sown directly but are generally better transplanted. All of this group of plants are susceptible to the soil-borne disease, clubroot. Once present in your garden soil, clubroot is ineradicable and will impose very serious limitations on your vegetable brassica production more or less indefinitely. Clubroot is often introduced into otherwise uncontaminated gardens in the roots or in the soil adhering to the roots of transplants. And because there can be no guarantee that transplants you buy are free from the disease, I would urge all gardeners to raise their own brassica plants if at all possible.

Perennials

The second big advantage of buying plants is of special importance with perennials. Here of course the value of the 'head start' is much greater (you will be a very patient gardener if you opt to raise your own trees or even bulb-forming plants from seed), but the choice in varieties is of even bigger significance. Many of the best types of herbaceous perennials and shrubs don't produce seeds; having double flowers (and hence no stamens), they have lost the ability to do so.

Conifers and other evergreens are invariably sold in containers

Even those with single or semi-double flowers are generally complex hybrids and bear seeds that give rise to a hotchpotch of plants, decidedly inferior to the parent; gardeners say that the offspring don't 'come true'. So all of these types must be propagated by vegetative means, generally by cuttings (page 30), and so buying a plant is your only way of obtaining new stock.

At garden centres, perennials that you buy will be in plastic containers. Check that they have compost filled close to the lip of the container and although ideally you should find no weed or moss growth, this is an unrealistic expectation. Small amounts of weed, moss and liverwort are tolerable but they and the top centimetre (half inch) of compost should always be scraped away before you plant.

25

GROWING PLANTS FROM SEED

66 *You won't have gardened for very long before you discover the huge satisfaction that comes from raising your own plants from seed. An old gardening friend, who had himself produced countless thousands of plants in this way, always used to refer to it, every year, as a miracle. Of course, no gardener raises all of his or her plants from seed; and nor can they because many varieties simply don't 'come true' (page 25). But starting with seed is almost essential for others and the operation falls neatly into two categories: that of seed sown indoors for transplanting, and that of sown directly into the garden.* 99

Hardy and half-hardy plants

Plants that originate in warm climates but can thrive perfectly well outdoors in our summers, although not our winters, are called half-hardy. Some of them (sunflowers and French marigolds for example) are naturally true annuals but most (petunias, lobelias and busy lizzies for instance) are, in reality, perennial. When grown in our gardens for one season only they all tend to be called half-hardy annuals and they must all be started off in warmth. And there are also some hardy plants (cauliflowers and bedding alyssum for instance) that benefit from the same type of indoor start to extend their growing season.

Sowing seed indoors

The 'indoors' most suitable for sowing seed is a greenhouse but can also be a conservatory, house window-sill or other place that is both light and warm. I have often reminded gardeners that plants require a higher temperature for their seeds to germinate than they ever require in their lives again. That slightly enhanced temperature may be satisfied simply by the indoor environment itself, or it may require something more. But in both cases, warmth often means dryness and as seeds must also have moisture to germinate, some device that cuts down water loss is essential. To meet these needs, you will need some kind of propagator. At its simplest, it can be a pot of compost covered with a plastic bag; at its rather more sophisticated and convenient, it is a plastic tray that has a removable, ventilated cover and stands on, or includes, some form of electric heating element.

Modern seed packets provide instructions, some sparse, some very good, detailing any special germination requirements that particular types might have. But in the absence of any other information, use a proprietary seedling compost, watered and then allowed to drain, sow the seeds thinly on the surface and then cover them lightly with more compost. Among common special requirements are the need to leave the seeds exposed on the surface of the compost (as with primulas).

Perhaps the most critical stage of all in the half-hardy annual technique is hardening off. Raised indoors in warmth, your seedlings will be very susceptible to damage from the widely fluctuating temperatures that occur outdoors, even in early summer. Hardening off is the process through which they are encouraged gradually to produce more resilient tissue. The best place for hardening off is in a cold frame into which the trays of seedlings are placed. I always allow at least two weeks for hardening off: in the first week, the frame cover is left half open in the day-time but closed up at night. In the second week, it is left fully open

You can raise you own seedlings with a simple propagator and divided trays

the daytime and half open at night. If you have no cold frame, trays or pots of seedlings may be put outside during the day and taken under cover at night although this is a laborious task and an inexpensive cold frame makes a very worthwhile investment.

Seed-sowing outdoors

For many garden plants, sowing seed directly outdoors into the garden soil makes more sense than sowing it in warmth, because they don't respond to being transplanted, because they are required in very large numbers and/or because they grow quickly enough outdoors.

Assuming that the planting area has been dug in advance, it should be raked about one week before sowing to remove any remaining large clods and at the same time, a general fertiliser should be scattered over and raked

Annual flower seeds are best scattered in marked out areas

into the upper few centimetres (the top inch) of the soil.

In most instances, seeds are sown in rows. The spacing between the rows varies with the type of seed as does the depth to which the seed channel or drill should be made (check the seed packet). A bamboo cane or the edge of a draw hoe will make a perfectly adequate seed drill. After sowing, carefully push back the soil over the drill with the back of the rake, taking care not to push the seeds out of the drill.

Sometimes it is necessary for seeds to be broadcast sown. Summer flowering annuals, for instance, will be needed in groups rather than straight lines and discrete areas within beds and borders should be prepared for them, the soil being carefully raked away for sowing and then raked back again afterwards.

Vegetable seeds should be sown in marked-out furrows or drills

GROWING BULBS, CORMS OR TUBERS

6 6 *Although botanically, they are very different, bulbs, corms, tubers and some types of rhizome have one very practical thing in common for gardeners: they are all structures in which plant food is stored. This means that they provide the plant with the means to survive below ground over winter, and also offer it a flying start (and the gardener almost certain results), when growth does recommence in the spring. You need skill not to obtain real success from mature bulbs, at least in the first year after planting.* 9 9

popular but relatively few types can compete sufficiently well with the grass to thrive. And even those bulbs suitable for growing in this way should never be planted in grass that is constantly mown. A sound principle is to leave the foliage of bulbous plants undisturbed

General considerations

Bulbous plants (and I use the term in its wide sense to include those with corms, tubers or swollen rhizomes too) vary enormously in size from tiny species suitable for the rock garden or containers, to giants that can only really be found a home at the back of a large border. There are types that require rich moist soil and others that need hot, impoverished conditions. Most are hardy and can be allowed to grow unmolested for years (this is usually referred to as naturalising them), although a few such as gladioli and dahlias are tender and must be lifted when their above ground growth has been killed back by frost. A very few, like the popular little yellow-flowered *Iris danfordiae* and also, in my experience, many of the large-flowered hybrid tulips, although in reality perennial, tend to decline in vigour and flower sparsely after the first season and are better treated as annuals.

Almost all bulbous plants, however, share one feature. Their swollen underground storage organ is liable to be damaged by pests and is also prone to attack by decay fungi in moist conditions, especially while it is dormant. A heavy clay soil is seldom ideal for them, although some localised improvement can be made when planting (see opposite). Growing bulbs in areas of grass is

Many bulbs are now sold loose by weight to enable you to select your own

By keeping your dahlia tubers every year, you can multiply your stock

for six weeks after the last flowers fade before cutting it down.

Buying and planting bulbous plants

Bulbous plants are sold widely by mail order and in garden centres where they can generally be bought in one of two ways: pre-packed or loose. Buying the bulbs pre-packed gives you a wider choice of varieties but if you want large numbers of the commoner types, then bulk buying is more economical. When selecting loose bulbs, avoid any that are split, undersized, mouldy and shrivelled; and if you find some abnormally large specimens with two, instead one 'nose' or point at the top, choose them as they will produce two flowers. I think that buying mixed varieties is a false

economy; the impact of the later-flowering types is inevitably diminished by them being surrounded by the dying flowers of the earlier ones.

Most reputable bulb suppliers now give full planting directions but there is still considerable confusion in gardeners' minds regarding planting depth. A good general rule is to place the bulb with its base at a depth in the soil equal to three times its diameter. Most importantly in clay, but also in a light soil, it is wise to lay in the bottom of the planting hole approximately 3–4cm (1¼–1½in) depth of sand to which a little bone meal has been added. This will minimise the likelihood of rotting. Cylindrical bulb planters work on the principle of removing a plug of soil to produce a hole into which bulbs can be placed. In practice, however, I have never found these easy to use and a trowel or spade is much easier.

Multiplying bulbous plants

Many bulbous plants may be multiplied by splitting up established clumps after a few years although young or 'daughter' bulbs may take a few years to reach flowering size. Gladioli and similar types that are lifted annually should have the tiny 'cormlets' pulled away and potted up for growing-on to plant out in due course while lily bulbs may be multiplied by removing two or three of the fleshy scales and potting them up in warmth. They too should reach flowering size in two or three years. In a few instances, such as dahlia tubers, softwood cuttings (page 30) may be removed from the over-wintered tubers in the early spring.

Gladiolus corms produce baby cormlets which can be removed and planted

MULTIPLYING YOUR PLANTS

❝ Although seed offers the simplest method of plant propagation, the various vegetative methods, most notably cuttings, layering and division are scarcely less satisfying. And they offer the only means of multiplying the many choice varieties of garden plant that either do not 'come true' from seed or, having double flowers, have lost the ability to produce any. ❞

Cuttings

There are three main types of cutting: softwood, semi-ripe and hardwood. The distinction between a softwood, semi-ripe and hardwood cutting reflects the age of the shoot from which it is removed and in general (a good rule of thumb), indicates the time of the year when they are best taken.

To take cuttings, tou will need a pair of secateurs, a very sharp knife or razor blade, some fresh hormone rooting powder, seedling and cutting or universal compost and some form of propagator. The simple seed tray/ plastic cover type of propagator is the most versatile. But do remember the cover; apart from hardwood cut-tings taken from deciduous plants in winter, all cuttings continue to lose water through their leaves at a time when they have no roots to compen-sate. Only by keeping the atmosphere around them moist, can the water loss be prevented and their survival assured.

A **softwood cutting** is one taken from a shoot of the current season's growth, complete with leaves, before hardening of the tissues.

A **semi-ripe cutting** is taken towards the end of the summer when the tissues have become springy.

A **hardwood cutting** is taken in late autumn or winter, when the plant is dormant.

For softwood and semi-ripe cuttings, cut shoots approximately 10cm (4in) long, remove the lower leaves, dip the shoot end in water, then in hormone rooting powder and place it about 2.5cm (1in) deep in moistened compost in a propagator. Line up the cuttings in the propagator tray (but try to ensure that their leaves do not touch each other), give them a gentle mist spray of water and place the cover over them. They should root in from two weeks to two months. Hardwood cuttings are better taken longer, about 25cm (10in), and simply pushed into prepared soil in a sheltered corner of the garden where they should root within six months.

Semi-ripe cuttings can often be pulled away from the parent plant

Layering

Layering is rather like taking cuttings but the shoot isn't cut from its parent until you know it has rooted. The plants for which it is most useful are large-leaved evergreens which continue to lose a great deal of water through their leaves if their shoots are taken as cuttings. Choose a fairly young shoot growing close to ground level and make a slit, about 5cm (2in) long, in the underside, cutting about one third of the way through the stem. Use a tiny sliver of match-stick to wedge open the slit and then dust the cut with rooting powder. Push it into the soil, use a wooden or stout galvanised metal peg to hold the shoot down, cover it with more soil and wait. It may take up to two seasons before sufficient roots

Softwood cuttings are taken from soft growth early in the season

more sense with many other types of herbaceous perennial to wait until the spring. Then, just as life is starting anew, you may be certain that any disturbance and check to growth won't be compounded by weeks of penetrating frost. With large clumps, it is best to divide by using two forks levered back to back but the very best tool for dividing smaller plants is a pair of strong hands, which will tear roots apart, not chop them. Most gardeners are usually satisfied with merely making two plants from one because they don't pull the clump apart sufficiently, but a good fist-sized piece of plant is best for replanting. Always remember to throw away the tough, woody and moribund material in the centre of the clump; start afresh with the young healthy growths from the periphery.

Hardwood cuttings are taken when the plants are dormant in winter

Small plants, like primulas, are best divided by hand

have formed for the shoot to manage an independent existence, but when it does, sever it cleanly from the parent.

Division

Finally, perhaps the simplest and most widely used propagation method of all is division, the straightforward process of cutting up one plant to produce more, or 'multiplying by dividing' as gardeners often call it. Autumn is the traditional season for division but while this might be satisfactory for such tough types as Michaelmas daisies, I have always found it makes much

BEDDING PLANTS AND ANNUALS

❛❛ *The term bedding plant denotes one use of hardy and half-hardy annuals: in providing colour in beds, principally during the summer. The individuals are massed together to provide colour patterns of varying complexity. Many municipal parks departments still plant large areas in public gardens in this way every year and these schemes can provide ideas you can adapt for your own garden, if this style of planting appeals to you. But it's important to realise that the bed of annuals is a thing of beauty and joy for a few months only. In the winter it is only as exciting as any other area of bare soil, so growing annuals as bedding to the exclusion of other types of plant is pretty unrewarding. My main message on these pages therefore is to encourage you to be more adventurous and grow annuals in other ways.* ❜❜

Other garden uses for annuals

Try using annuals as edging around a mixed border or interspersed between perennials. I also find that, used in moderation, they can add a great deal of interest to the kitchen garden; the combination of dark blue lobelia and fresh green parsley for instance is particularly appealing. But perhaps the greatest value of annuals comes with containers, for they are the mainstay of the hanging basket, window box and tub (page 54). They are planted in the spring and early summer to replace biennials or bulbs and they are removed in the autumn when the new biennials, bulbs or the two or three types of winter-flowering bedding plant (most notably winter flowering pansies and primulas) go in.

Although I have referred and shall continue to refer to these plants as annuals, many of them are perennials that we happen to grow as annuals; and while some of them are hardy, many (especially the potential perennials) are not. So some can be raised from seed sown directly outdoors, but most can't.

Annuals are very valuable for filling in gaps in perennial borders

I have included here the relatively few ornamental garden biennials (sown in one year to flower the next) because they complement annuals in providing colour at other times of the season.

Many types of annual are offered by seed companies only as mixtures; but in most cases, these mixtures are my second choice. To my mind there is no doubt that the best and prettiest plantings, of whatever type, can only be made with individually coloured varieties. Only when you can predict which colours will appear in which place can the most attractive planting schemes be made.

With experience, you could try carpet bedding using coloured foliage

As with vegetables (page 58), you will see varieties of some annuals designated as F1 hybrids. But in the formal bedding scheme, at least, there is considerable merit in the uniformity that the F1 hybrid offers.

I have already discussed raising plants from seed and buying them, ready for planting, from garden centres or nurseries. But for those gardeners who prefer to undertake at least part of the plant raising themselves (or who, for various reasons, can't or don't want to be bothered with seed sowing), the major seed companies now have ways to help you. They now offer young seedlings, 'plantlets' or 'plug plants' at various stages of growth from newly germinated onwards for you to continue to raise yourself. Understandably, supplies are limited by their production capacity so order well in advance.

Soil preparation

When planting an entire bed with annuals, the soil should be prepared in much the same way as it would be for vegetables (page 58). Where they are simply to be slotted in amongst other types of plant, this is more difficult but always prepare the soil as thoroughly as possible and incorporate a dressing of general purpose fertiliser. Once growth is under way in the summer, annuals will require constant attention to watering and will not give of their best unless they are provided with liquid fertiliser at least once every fortnight. Dead-heading too will help ensure an attractive appearance and the continuing production of new blooms. Pests and diseases are seldom serious, although mildew can take its toll in dry summers, encouraged by the almost inevitable close planting.

Bedding plants offer some of gardening's brightest colours

RECOMMENDED EASY-TO-GROW ANNUALS AND BIENNIALS

Acroclinium Everlasting flower
Ageratum Floss flower
Antirrhinum Snapdragon
Begonia
Brachyscome iberidifolia Swan River daisy
Calendula officinalis Pot marigold
Callistephus chinensis Aster
Campanula isophylla Bell flower
Chrysanthemum (annual varieties)
Clarkia/Godetia
Cosmos
Dahlia
Delphinium (annual species) Larkspur
Dianthus Pinks, carnations
Dianthus barbatus Sweet William
Dimorphotheca Star of the veld
Dorotheanus Livingstone daisy
Erysimum species Wallflower
Eschscholzia Californian poppy

Gaillardia
Gazania
Gypsophila elegans Baby's breath
Helianthus annuus Sunflower
Helichrysum Everlasting flower
Iberis species Candytuft
Impatiens Busy Lizzie
Lavatera
Limnanthes douglasii Poached egg plant
Linaria Toadflax
Lobelia
Lobularia maritima Alyssum
Matthiola (or *Malcolmia*) species Stock
Matricaria eximia
Molucella laevis Bells of Ireland
Nemesia
Nicotiana Ornamental tobacco plant
Nigella damascena Love-in-a-mist

Ornamental grasses
Papaver species Poppy
Pelargonium Half-hardy geranium
Petunia
Phlox drummondii
Primula
Reseda odorata Mignonette
Rhodanthe (or *Helipterum*) Everlasting flower
Rudbeckia Cone flower
Salpiglossis
Salvia
Scabiosa species Scabious
Tagetes species Marigolds and tagetes
Tithonia Mexican sunflower
Viola species Pansies and violas
Zinnia

PERENNIALS

Herbaceous perennials are both beautiful and indispensable but lie some way behind shrubs (although well ahead of annuals) in their requirements for continuing attention. The name perennial indicates that they may be left undisturbed for many years, but I must stress that being perennial does not equate with being immortal. After four or five years, almost all types of herbaceous perennial will require rejuvenation through division. Being not only perennial but also herbaceous means that the plants die down to a clump of roots and, above ground, a mass of dead stems. And the herbaceous nature of the above ground structure leads to the most labour demanding aspect of herbaceous perennial gardening for, in many instances, they require some form of support.

Using perennials in the garden

Like annuals, most herbaceous perennials (the evergreen types being the exceptions) offer you little or nothing in the winter so must be used with care; being generally large plants, the gap they leave out of season is also a large one. In modern gardens, therefore, herbaceous perennials are seldom planted in beds or borders to the exclusion of other plants. Most commonly, they are integrated with shrubs in mixed borders (page 36). Even here, it's important to select varieties with complementary colours and flowering times and to choose carefully the taller varieties for planting at the back and sides of the border with the lower-growing ones in the centre and front.

Perennials are especially valuable when used with shrubs in a mixed border

Obtaining perennials

Seed catalogues have large sections devoted to herbaceous perennials and it may be appear, therefore, that the best way to raise them is from seed. In general, I find that it isn't. Largely I say this because the best (in the sense of most attractive or functionally useful) varieties can't usually be raised in this manner. They must be propagated vegetatively and thus must be purchased from nurseries or garden centres as plants.

Planting

When planting any herbaceous perennials, follow the same general technique as I have outlined for trees and shrubs (page 36), ensuring that the prepared planting hole has a volume approximately twice that of the plant's root ball. If you are planting or replanting an entire border from scratch, it makes sense to double dig it (page 10).

Care

Apart from routine staking and fairly regular division, herbaceous perennials require feeding twice a year with a general-purpose balanced fertiliser such as blood, fish and bone. Water in dry spells and, following the first feeding, and while the soil is still moist, apply a thick organic mulch around the plants or, if you have sufficient organic matter available, over the entire bed.

In the early autumn, the above ground growth should be cut down and composted. Where dead heads remain with masses of seeds or where the dead stems have a particularly

Shaded borders require a careful choice of plants; ferns are especially useful

Ornamental grasses are beautiful

attractive appearance, leave them in place for birds to feed on.

The relatively close planting of herbaceous perennials that achieves the dramatic effect of massed blooms means that they can be prone to pests and diseases. Among pests, aphids are especially troublesome, while among diseases, mildew can be very damaging especially in a dry summer. So try not to mass your plants together too closely to permit the air to circulate.

RECOMMENDED EASY-TO-GROW HERBACEOUS PERENNIALS

Acanthus Bear's breech
Achillea
Aconitum
Alchemilla mollis Lady's mantle
Althaea Hollyhock
Anemone x hybrida
Aquilegia Columbine
Artemisia Wormwood
Aster Michaelmas daisy
Astilbe
Astrantia
Bergenia
Calamintha
Campanula Bell flower
Centranthus Valerian
Chrysanthemum
Cimicifuga
Clematis
Delphinium

Digitalis Foxglove
Doronicum Leopard's bane
Euphorbia Spurge
Fern
Filipendula Meadow sweet
Geranium Cranesbills
Geum
Gypsophila Baby's breath
Helenium
Helleborus
Hemerocallis Day lily
Heuchera
Hosta
Iris
Kniphofia Red-hot poker
Lamium Dead-nettle
Lavatera Tree mallow
Ligularia
Lupinus Lupin

Lychnis Catchfly
Lysimachia Loosestrife
Lythrum salicaria Purple loosestrife
Malva Mallow
Meconopsis Blue poppy
Nepeta
Perennial Grasses
Phlox
Polygonatum Solomon's seal
Polygonum
Primula
Pulmonaria Lungwort
Rudbeckia Black-eyed susan
Schizostylis
Thalictrum Meadow rue
Trollius hybrids Globe flower
Verbascum Mullein

SHRUBS

66 You will find shrubs indispensable in your garden, whatever its size, and I believe they are the most important of all the types of plant available for today's gardener. If you choose carefully from the huge range of deciduous and evergreen varieties available, it's possible to have attractive flowers, foliage, bark, buds and overall shape all year round. There are shrubs for almost any soil and any site and, overall, you will find they require less attention than either annuals or herbaceous perennials. 99

Coloured foliage can be effective

Using shrubs in the garden

In times past, shrubs were grown almost exclusively in a shrubbery, a planting that generally contained relatively few different types and, in the 19th century at least, was heavily dependent on rather sombre evergreens. All has now changed, however, and a planting dedicated to shrubs in the modern garden, even a fairly small modern garden, can offer appeal in every month of the year. But shrubs are of greater value in the mixed border, where they are interspersed with herbaceous perennials and possibly some annuals and bulbs too. The shrubs will provide a permanent framework and, therefore, visual appeal even

when the other plants have died down in winter. Many shrubs also make excellent subjects for growing in containers (see page 54).

Obtaining shrubs

Shrubs are most readily bought from garden centres and nurseries in containers during the growing season. My advice is to visit your garden centre regularly and buy plants that take your eye as each comes into bloom or other seasonal appeal. In this way you will soon build up a collection of year-round interest. Subsequently, as you read about and want different or more

unusual shrubs, you will probably have to buy them by mail order. They will almost certainly then be delivered in the dormant season after being lifted from the ground; then described as bare-rooted, they should be planted as soon as possible.

Planting

Dig a hole of volume approximately twice that of the root ball of the shrub and pile the soil at the side. Then mix with this a similar volume of well rotted manure or garden compost (or proprietary planting mixture) and several

Flowering shrubs will enhance a planting of herbaceous perennials

Solo shrubs make striking features

handfuls of bone meal. Break up the soil in the base of the hole with a fork then gradually refill, pressing it down gently with your boot until the remaining hole is deep enough for the shrub's roots to be spread out in it, while leaving the original soil mark on the stem level with the soil surface. With a container grown plant, tease away some of the roots around the sides and bottom of the compost ball as you place it in the hole. Then gradually fill in around the roots with the soil and organic matter mixture, pressing down gently with your boot. Water the area around the plant very thoroughly, then finally, make a small mound of manure or compost around the base of the shrub, sloping down and away from the stems.

Care

Feed at least once during the early part of the season with a general purpose or rose fertiliser (the former for foliage, the latter for flowering varieties). Mulch early in the spring and when shrubs are planted in lawns, leave an area of bare soil of approximately 1m (3ft) in diameter around the base, on which mulch and fertiliser may be applied.

Pests and diseases are less important on shrubs. Aphids may attack young shoots, roots can decay in wet soil, foliage may be disfigured by mildew and cankers, diseases may attack branches.

RECOMMENDED EASY-TO-GROW SHRUBS

Abutilon	Cotinus Smoke bush	Kerria	Potentilla
Acer Maple	Cotoneaster	Kolkwitzia	Prunus Ornamental cherry
Aralia	Cytisus Broom	Laurus Laurel	Pyracantha Firethorn
Arbutus Strawberry tree	Daphne	Lavandula Lavender	Rhamnus Buckthorn
Arctostaphylos Bearberry	Deutzia	Lavatera Tree mallow	Rhododendron
Aucuba Spotted laurel	Elaeagnus	Leucothoe	Rhus Sumac
Berberis	Erica Heath, heather	Leycesteria Himalayan	Ribes Flowering currant
Brachyglottis	Escallonia	honeysuckle	Romneya Californian
Buddleja	Euonymus x fatshedera	Ligustrum Privet	tree poppy
Buxus Box	Fatsia	Lonicera Honeysuckle	Rosmarinus Rosemary
Callicarpa	Forsythia	Magnolia	Rubus Ornamental bramble
Callistemon Bottle brush	Fothergilla	Mahonia	Ruscus Butcher's broom
Calluna Heather	Fuchsia	Myrtus Myrtle	Salix Willow
Camellia	Garrya	Neillia	Sambucus Elder
Ceanothus	Gaultheria	Olearia	Santolina Cotton lavender
Ceratostigma Shrubby	Griselinia	Ononis	Sarcococca
plumbago	Halimium	Osmanthus	Skimmia
Chaenomeles Ornamental	Hamamelis Witch hazel	Pachysandra	Spartium Broom
quince	Hebe Shrubby veronica	Paeonia Tree paeony	Spiraea
Chimonanthus Winter	Helianthemum Rock rose	Pernettya	Symphoricarpos Snowberry
sweet	Helichrysum	Perovskia Russian sage	Syringa Lilac
Choisya Mexican orange	Hibiscus	Philadelphus Mock orange	Tamarix Tamarisk
blossom	Hippophae Sea buckthorn	Phlomis Jerusalem sage	Ulex Gorse
Cistus Broom	Hydrangea	Phormium New Zealand	Vaccinium Bilberry
Cornus Dogwood	Hypericum St John's wort	flax	Viburnum
Corokia	Ilex Holly	Photinia	Vinca Periwinkle
Coronilla	Indigofera	Pieris	Weigela
Corylus Hazel	Jasminum Jasmine	Pittosporum	Yucca

ROSES

" The days have gone when almost every garden contained a large bed of roses although I'm sure they do remain one of the best-loved flowers. There's certainly no doubt that the range of available varieties, with high levels of resistance to the diseases that have plagued roses in the past, means that gardeners have never had a better choice than they do today. So even if the traditional rose bed doesn't appeal to you, I hope you will find room for one or two plants; and I hope, too, that I can convince you of their great versatility. "

Types of roses and how to use them in the garden

The bed devoted to roses, like these floribundas, is becoming less popular

There must be half-a-dozen different ways of subdividing the huge number of rose varieties but I shall use what seems to me the most useful for the gardener choosing roses for the first time.

Modern bush roses

These are the types that you will see massed in public parks and other fairly formal settings. They are divided into hybrid teas (or, as they now tend to be called, large-flowered roses) which generally have one rather large bloom at the end of each stem and often some perfume; and floribundas (or cluster-flowered roses) which have a group of smaller blooms and often less scent. Use them in beds on their own or dotted among other shrubs in a mixed border.

Shrub roses

These are flowering shrubs that also just happen to be roses. They are often, but not always, tall growing, need very little pruning and often have a delicious perfume. Most flower for a short season, although a group called the English roses cleverly combines the fragrance and flower form of the old varieties with the longer season of the modern types. If you have room, you can devote a bed exclusively to shrub roses but they are better used as specimens within a larger planting.

Patio and miniature roses

Miniature roses and the slightly taller patio roses are dwarf bush roses but because they are so small, they need very little pruning and are ideal for planting around terraces or even in pots.

Standard roses

Standard roses are usually bush varieties that have been grafted on top of a single stem although shrub and even climbing varieties can be used in this way too; some of the climbers form lovely weeping standards. Standard roses make excellent features in the centre of beds or other areas.

Climbing roses

Climbing roses are mostly varieties of one or other of the main rose groups that happen to grow very tall and usually very quickly. So there are climbing hybrid teas, climbing floribundas and even some climbing miniatures. The scope for using climbing roses in a garden is enormous: the less vigorous ones can be trained up trellis at the side of your front door, others can scramble a little more adventurously over the porch or perhaps over a

A good way to display roses is to put them in borders with other shrubs

wooden archway or pergola while the vigorous monsters can be allowed free rein up an old apple tree where they will rapidly take over the crown.

Obtaining roses

Rose may be bought in much the same way as other flowering shrubs (page 36) but the variety available in containers will always be a very small fraction of the whole range. I do advise you, therefore, to visit a rose nursery in the height of summer if possible so you can make your selection from plants in bloom for delivery later in the year.

Planting and care

As with all plants, roses have their preferences for soil and site. The most important requirement is a moisture retentive soil; a clayey soil provides this naturally but even a light soil will grow perfectly good roses if lots of compost or other organic matter is forked in.

The key to good roses is good feeding and I give them a proprietary rose fertiliser in the spring, immediately after pruning, and then again after the first flowers fade in early summer.

Pruning is dealt with in some detail on pages 84–7 but a simple rule of thumb for the main groups of roses is: on hybrid teas, cut back all shoots by roughly half, slightly more for weak-growing types, slightly less for strong ones; on floribundas, cut out one-third of all shoots each spring and cut back the remainder by one-third of their length; on shrubs, simply cut out any very old or diseased shoots, sufficient to keep the centre of the plant from being congested.

Problems

There are four main troubles on roses, but all are easy to treat provided you act at the first signs of damage: aphids, mildew, blackspot and rust. Products are available which combine insecticide and fungicide in one spray, but more detailed information is given in *Best Garden Doctor*.

Climbing roses still have no rival for covering an archway

CLIMBING PLANTS

" The advice given to the would-be adventurer and seeker after fortune in the 19th century was 'Go west, young man'. The advice I give to the would-be gardener and seeker after horticultural satisfaction today is 'Go up, young man (or woman)'. Forget the notion that gardening is a two-dimensional pursuit; forget the idea that a small garden has an area of only x or y square metres. Gardens are to be measured not by area but by volume. Ignore the vertical third dimension and you ignore climbing plants and a huge amount of visual delight and practical satisfaction. "

Using climbers in the garden

Climbers differ from other types of shrub in that they have weak stems and must therefore be supported in some way; either by growing them over other plants, much as they grow naturally, or more formally training

Painted obelisks are back in fashion

them up artificial supports such as trellises, fences, archways or pergolas. The unashamedly artificial supports are most appropriate for the small or formal garden, leaving the more natural 'free rein' approach to larger and preferably fairly well wooded gardens.

Climbing plants climb in several rather different ways and these dictate the type of support they require. Some merely twine themselves around their supports; sometimes it is the stem (as in wisteria) and sometimes the leaf stalk (as in clematis) that fulfils this role and there is inexplicable variation between different plants in their tendency for twining clockwise or anticlockwise. Other species (like many of the popular *Parthenocissus* vines) have stem ends or leaf stalks modified to form specialised grasping tendrils while a few, ivies most notably, have modified aerial roots with minute suckers. It's important to remember that these so-called self-clinging plants can damage old bricks and mortar although they can safely be grown on modern buildings. All climbers should, however, be trimmed

Wisteria is still the most wonderful climber for a house wall

A natural setting for honeysuckles

back before they grow beneath roof tiles or through window frames.

Many types of climber are naturally woodland plants and many therefore are fairly shade tolerant although you should be aware that some also have a requirement for shade at the roots but will only flower satisfactorily if their upper parts are in full sun.

Obtaining climbers

My comments on shrubs (page 36) are relevant to climbers too but don't forget that there is an important group of annual and herbaceous climbers, most of which can be raised from seed.

Planting

As with other types of garden ornamental, there are climbers adapted to most types of soil but they benefit greatly from careful soil preparation before planting. This is because the soil at the base of a wall, hedge, fence, tree or other support is almost inevitably dry and often impoverished too.

I have included here a selection of good perennial and annual types. You will find a greater range described in detail in *Best Climbers* although if clematis are your particular favourites, they are dealt with comprehensively in *Best Clematis*.

Actinidia kolomikta deciduous, attractively patterned leaves, twining.
Aristolochia macrophylla Dutchman's pipe, deciduous, twining, curious flowers.
Campsis radicans Trumpet vine, deciduous self clinging, exotic orange-red flowers.
Clematis mainly deciduous, twining, a huge range of varieties.
Eccremocarpus scaber Glory vine, evergreen, best grown as an annual, small red/orange flowers.
Fallopia baldschuanica Russian vine, mile-a-minute vine, deciduous, twining, very vigorous

Hedera Ivy, evergreen, self-clinging.
Humulus Ornamental hop, herbaceous deciduous perennial.
Hydrangea petiolaris Climbing hydrangea, deciduous, self-clinging.
Ipomoea Morning glory, herbaceous, best grown as an annual.
Lathyrus Sweet pea, most grown as annuals but perennial species exist.
Lonicera Honeysuckle, deciduous and evergreen, twining, many very fragrant.
Parthenocissus Virginia creeper and relatives, deciduous self-clinging.
Passiflora caerulea Passion flower, more or less evergreen, tendrils, exotic flowers.
Tropaeolum Climbing nasturtiums, and Canary creeper. Best grown as annuals, red, orange, yellow flowers.
Vitis Vine, deciduous, more or less self-clinging, edible grapevine and also varieties with ornamental foliage.
Wisteria deciduous, twining, vigorous.

The addition of plentiful organic matter, regular feeding (using liquid fertilisers during the growing season) and watering are, therefore, most important. Place the plant about 20cm (8in) away from the support itself, following the directions that I have given for shrub planting (page 36).

Care and problems

The more formally trained climbers require regular attention to pruning and training and also to tying-in to their supports (see page 87 and also my book *Best Pruning*). Care must be taken to ensure that the support ties are checked annually; a rapidly growing climber such as a wisteria grows considerably in girth too and a wire that was loose in one autumn can be almost a garrotte by the next.

Largely because of the shelter afforded by the supports, climbing plants as a group tend to be rather prone to pests and diseases; the shelter and warmth that we give to the plants affects the problems too. Among pests, red spider mite and aphids are troublesome, while among diseases, mildew will require watching carefully and probably need regular control.

41

BULBS

Although there are many gardens unsuited to annuals, some unsuited to herbaceous perennials and trees, and possibly a few unsuited to shrubs, I don't believe there is a garden anywhere that can't be enhanced by some bulbous plants. The reasons are two-fold: first that flowering success is all but guaranteed, certainly for the first season after planting, and second, although all share a swollen basal structure (sometimes a true bulb, sometimes not), the range of plant types that the group embraces is a very large one, so there is a bulbous plant that will fit in with any surroundings.

Using bulbous plants in the garden

On page 28, I described the way to obtain bulbs and also outlined the most reliable way to plant them. Here, I want to concentrate in a little more detail on the ways in which they can be used most effectively in your garden.

Formal bulb-only beds

If you visit municipal parks and other public gardens, you will see beds, often very large ones, given over solely to spring flowering bulbous plants, especially tulips and hyacinths. The impact can be very eye-catching and sometimes very pretty. It isn't, however, a type of planting that I suggest you adopt in your own garden unless you have a great deal of time and money to spare. The effect will be short lived: the flowering period of each variety is only about two weeks and trying to prolong this by using mixed varieties will diminish rather than enhance the result. This is because the later-flowering plants will inevitably vie for attention with the dead blooms of the earlier-flowering types. And they will all will need lifting and storing to make way for summer bedding plants after their brief flush of glory is over. There are better ways to use your garden space and better places to plant your bulbs.

and, among the larger spring-flowering bulbs, daffodils and narcissi will offer much the best results. Among smaller bulbs, species tulips, large-flowered Dutch crocus, leucojums, snowdrops and aconites are also generally very reliable. Do check the packet label or catalogue information carefully because some varieties, even of daffodil, are less successful. Bulbs for naturalising may be planted in areas of bare soil

Daffodils bring colour to borders early in the season

Informal bulb-only plantings

If you do like the idea of having areas planted exclusively with bulbs, you should select those types that don't require lifting annually, but will continue to grow and multiply naturally in the garden year after year. This method of growing bulbs is called naturalising them. The large-flowered hybrid tulips and hyacinths aren't especially suitable

or in grassy places, provided the grass can be left unmown for at least six weeks after the bulbs have flowered; this rules out lawns.

Other places where bulbs (small ones especially) may be planted and left undisturbed very successfully are in rock gardens, gravel beds, beneath trees and deciduous shrubs and similar places where the soil itself is not likely to be dug or disturbed frequently.

Dutch crocuses are ideally suited to growing in grass

Containers

Perhaps the most important role of all for bulbs is in containers. I discuss the choice and setting up of containers and the way they may be used in gardens on page 54, but for every type of container there is a suitable bulbous plant. In containers, the bulbs such as tulips and hyacinths that I dismissed as inappropriate for open garden plantings, really come into their own, because in most gardens, most containers are themselves temporary plantings. Hanging baskets, window boxes, tubs for terraces are all used to best effect when replanted in spring and autumn. The bulbs can, therefore, take their place alongside summer, spring and winter bedding, as appropriate.

An alternative planting idea is to use a larger container (a wooden half-barrel is ideal) and plant the bulbs in layers: the larger bulbs in the deepest layers

RECOMMENDED EASY-TO-GROW BULBOUS PLANTS

Agapanthus African lily
Allium Ornamental onion
Anemone
Arum Arum lily
Bulbocodium Red crocus
Cardiocrinum Giant lily
Chionodoxa Glory of the snow
Colchicum Naked ladies, meadow
 saffron
Corydalis
Crinum
Crocosmia Montbretia
Crocus
Cyclamen
Eranthis Winter aconite
Eremurus Foxtail lily
Erythronium Dog's tooth violet
Fritillaria Fritillary, crown imperial
Gagea
Galanthus Snowdrops

Galtonia Summer hyacinth
Gladiolus
Hyacinthoides Bluebell
Hyacinthus Hyacinth
Ipheion
Iris
Leucojum Snowflakes
Muscari Grape hyacinths
Narcissus Daffodils and narcissi
Nerine
Ornithogalum Star of bethlehem
Puschkinia
Schizostylis
Scilla Squills
Sternbergia
Trillium Wood lily
Triteleia
Tritonia
Tulipa Tulips
Zantedeschia Arum lily

Lilies are excellent container subjects

and one or two more layers, at staggered placings and shallower depths above them. I have just such a planting at the front of my own house every year; deeply planted narcissi emerge first, followed by shallowly planted crocus and, finally, the intermediate planting of tulips.

Last, but far from least, I must mention those most glorious of all bulbs, lilies. Many gardeners, especially new gardeners imagine that they are difficult and unreliable, and perhaps prone to pests and diseases. So they can be if they are planted in the open garden. But grow them as I grow all of mine in containers, and you will have very little trouble. They stay in the pots for several years until they become so congested that the clumps require dividing.

43

TREES

" More people have more problems in their garden through (very often their own choice of) trees than with anything else. The reasons aren't hard to find: trees are big, they grow slowly, they take up a great deal of space, they have an impact far beyond their immediate growing position, and their removal can be difficult, is often costly and may occasionally require legal permission. Inexperienced gardeners should therefore give greater attention to these two pages than to any others in the book. "

Using trees in the garden

Most people don't plant trees in groups; if you are very lucky and have sufficient space, you might conceivably plant a small copse but very few people have room for a wood. Trees must, therefore, be assessed as individuals rather than collectively. In most gardens a new tree (I shall have a few remarks about existing trees shortly) is likely to be used as a focal point as it will be larger than any other plant in your garden. There is no strict division between small trees and big shrubs but, by convention, anything that is likely to reach a height greater than 6m (20ft) on a single stem is called a tree.

Most small gardens have room for only one, carefully placed tree

When choosing this, ultimately, rather obvious and dominant addition to your garden, the following are the more important features that you should consider.

Size: check carefully, with at least two reference books (as estimates can vary widely), the ultimate height, and don't plant the tree closer to your house than a distance equal to one-and-a-half times this distance.

Leaves: is the tree deciduous or evergreen? There are far fewer hardy evergreens and although they will give cover and shelter all year round, this can be monotonous. The leaves of deciduous trees change in size, sometimes shape and often colour as they emerge, grow and then drop in the autumn. Look at the size of the leaves. Large leaves may be attractive while on the tree but can cause problems and hazards when they drop.

Bark, twigs and buds: what is the appearance of the trees when the leaves have fallen? Is the branch framework attractive in its own right or are the branches stark and ugly? Does the bark have an attractive colour (and remember that this too can change during the season and during the life of the trees); and are there attractive buds?

Flowers: most trees bear flowers; *en masse* they are usually called blossom and many trees for small gardens are sold and bought on this criterion alone. Blossom, however, lasts at most for a few weeks; does the plant offer enough attractive appeal for the remainder of the year?

Fruit: ornamental fruits (often called berries) are, by their nature, generally only present towards the end of the season and (bird life permitting), into the winter. Are the fruits attractive enough for the tree to be chosen for them alone? Most trees produce red fruit so those offering orange, white, pink or some other colour might be worth special consideration. And do the fruits arise from equally attractive blossom; remember that to be able to produce fruits, a tree must have single or at most semi-double flowers.

Planting and care of garden trees

Trees may be planted following the guidelines that I have given for shrubs (page 36) but with one significant difference. Until their stems are strong enough to provide them with full support, trees require staking.

Stakes should always be placed on the side of the stem facing the prevailing wind (so the stem is blown away from and not on to it) and secured with purpose made belt-pattern ties. Please don't use wire for tying.

Removal of a tree should really be the last resort and even a very large specimen that is casting deep shade or otherwise creating difficulties can often be saved. But do remember that the pruning or removal of large trees should be performed by a qualified professional operator, who will not only be familiar with the techniques and equipment necessary, but will also have third party insurance.

Given space, a small copse of ornamental trees makes a lovely feature

How to deal with existing trees

Very few ornamental trees require routine pruning and the subject only really arises when they become large and old. In general, I have to say that a tree in need of pruning because of its size has been planted in the wrong place (see page 86). The appearance of fungal fruiting bodies on the branches of a tree indicate decay of the wood within and where such growths arise on the main trunk, the suggestion must be that the decay is already extensive. Expert advice should be sought, therefore, if there is any likelihood that damage to property will ensue if the entire tree or some of its branches fall in a gale.

Trees planted close to buildings can soon outgrow the available space

SOME RECOMMENDED TREES FOR SMALL AND MEDIUM-SIZED GARDENS

Acacia Silver wattle, Mimosa	*Cornus* Dogwood	*Liquidamber* Sweet gum	*Prunus* Flowering cherries
Acer Maples	*Crataegus* Thorn	*Magnolia*	*Pyrus* Ornamental pear
Amelanchier Snowy mespil	*Eucalyptus* Gum tree	*Malus* Crab apple	*Robinia* False acacia
Caragana Pea tree	*Gleditsia* Honey locust	*Parrotia*	*Salix* Willow (some)
Catalpa Indian bean tree	*Ilex* Holly	*Paulownia* Foxglove tree	*Sorbus* Mountain ash
Cercis Judas tree	*Laburnum*	*Photinia*	*Syringa* Lilac

HEDGES

" The hedge is almost certainly the most under-appreciated of all garden features. Far too often, a hedge of uncertain quality simply forms part of the boundary of a garden, cut once or twice each year but otherwise given little thought. I hope to persuade you that hedges can be both interesting and very beautiful; and that they don't have to be restricted to the edges of your garden. "

What is a hedge?

This might seem an obvious question but it is one that gardeners seldom ask themselves; so they seldom realise that hedges are basically long, very narrow woods that are subject to pretty strict

Flowering hedges can be very beautiful but are less dense

For a dense, symmetrical hedge, nothing beats well clipped yew

management. Yet most of the plants used for hedges are trees and if neglected, they will grow tall and very tree-like, hence much of the furore surrounding that very vigorous conifer, the Leyland cypress. It is not a very fast growing plant, it is a very fast-growing tree and like every other tree used for hedging, it must be cut regularly. The faster growing the hedge plant, the quicker will it reach the desired height but the more frequently must it be cut to maintain that height. There are other analogies with tree care too. The better prepared the planting position, the better will the hedge become established. And the greater the care given to weed control, feeding and watering, especially in the early years, the better will be the hedge in the long term.

The use of hedges in the garden

It can't be denied that most hedges in most gardens do form part of the garden boundary. Where a boundary is needed quickly, as it often is to provide privacy in a new garden, don't simply reject a hedge in favour of the instant effect that a fence will provide. Use the fence to provide protection for a young hedge planted alongside; by the time that the hedge has reached the desired height of about 2m (6½ft), the fence will probably be coming to the end of its life.

Do consider using hedges within the garden too. They can be used to subdivide your plot to create discrete areas, each with a different character; short lengths of ornamental hedge can be positioned as individual, free-standing features, much as large shrubs can; and dwarf hedges can be used very attractively and effectively to border kitchen gardens or formal beds. And in less formal gardens, hedges of native species will provide invaluable cover and a habitat for wildlife.

Planting the hedge

Prepare the planting position as for any other tree or shrub (page 36), although digging and manuring a trench rather than individual planting holes will immeasurably aid root spread and rapidity of growth and anchorage.

Buy the best quality hedging plants you can afford. If you are only planting a short run, then choose large, container-grown specimens, but if you need large numbers, you should buy them bare-rooted from a wholesale nursery. The planting distance will vary with species, but tall plants will always benefit from staking in the early stages. Where a particularly thick hedge is needed, it is worth planting a staggered double row of plants.

Cutting and other care

Use good stainless steel hand shears, kept oiled and sharp, or the best powered trimmers that you can afford. For most garden hedges, powered trimmers with 35–40cm (1¼–1½ft) blades will be adequate. For very long hedges or those above about 1.5m (5ft) tall, however, 45cm will be very much more useful. Always wear protective goggles and strong but flexible gloves when working. After planting a new hedge,

do not wait until the plants have attained the desired ultimate height before you start to cut. Trim them a little each year (cutting away approximately one-third of the previous

season's growth) to encourage bushiness. Thereafter, hedges should be cut in early summer and again in early autumn. All hedge trimmings can be shredded to make excellent compost.

RECOMMENDED HEDGING PLANTS

Berberis
Buxus Box
Carpinus Hornbeam
Chamaecyparis lawsoniana Lawson cypress
Corylus Hazel
Cotoneaster
Crataegus Hawthorn
x Cupressocyparis leylandii Leyland cypress (large exposed gardens only)
Escallonia
Fagus Beech
Forsythia
Hippophae Sea buckthorn

Ilex Holly
Lavandula Lavender
Ligustrum Privet
Lonicera nitida
Prunus Blackthorn, plums, sloe
Prunus laurocerasus Laurel
Pyracantha Firethorn
Ribes sanguineum Flowering currant
Rosa Rose
Rosmarinus Rosemary
Spiraea
Symphoricarpos Snowberry
Taxus Yew
Thuja plicata

For rural gardens, hawthorn is both tough and stock-proof

LAWNS

❝ Are gardeners still judged by the quality of their lawns? There's no doubt that the presence of stripes still unaccountably carries a great deal of gardening kudos, even though it is now far easier to produce them than ever it was in the past. The range of aids now available to gardeners to produce and care for lawns is enormous, so I can't think there is really an excuse for anyone not to have the lawn of their desires, if not their dreams. ❞

Allow some grass to grow longer to reduce work and add interest

Creating a lawn

In an ideal world, the area for a new lawn should be dug and prepared by incorporating organic matter in advance, much as it is for other types of plant, but the size of the area involved usually makes this degree of thoroughness impracticable. Nonetheless, especially on a virgin site, use a rotary cultivator both to turn over the soil and then to break it down into a finer tilth.

The site needn't be flat; a gentle slope can be very attractive but as it is extremely difficult to remove extensive humps and hollows once a lawn is established, care in grading the site to obtain a flat or uniformly sloping surface beforehand will repay dividends. After grading, the whole site must be levelled and firmed. The most effective tool for levelling and removing stones and clods of soil is the spring-tine lawn rake; but take care to rake alternately in two directions at right angles or you may introduce and accentuate rather than diminish any humps and hollows. About a week before you lay the lawn, scatter autumn lawn fertiliser over the area; use the same fertiliser even if you are doing the job in spring because it's important to use a blend relatively low in nitrogen.

So far, the preparation is the same whether you use turf or seed and the choice between the two is most likely to be made on grounds of cost. Seed is certainly cheaper but it is much more chancy for the inexpert and also very much slower to give you an end result. I would now almost always opt for specially grown turf which is available nation wide.

If you do use seed, choose a warm, moist and fairly windless day. Most seed companies provide some form of measure or dosing device to indicate the amount of seed to apply per square metre and you will find this easiest to use if you divide up your prepared area

A neatly clipped and mown lawn instantly gives order to a garden

with canes and string into metre (yard) squares. After sowing, rake very lightly over the area and then firm the soil with the back of a rake. Suspend light-weight plastic netting over the newly sown seeds to protect them from birds.

Turves should be laid off-set from each other, like bricks in a wall. Lay a plank on which to stand as you work, and tamp the new turves down with the back of a rake. Never try to lay small pieces of turf at the edges; always move a larger piece to the edge and insert infilling pieces towards the centre. The edge may then be trimmed with a half-moon edging knife. After sowing or turfing, apply water by sprinkler at regular intervals to ensure that the soil is not allowed to dry out. If you have sown seed, use a very fine spray in order not to wash the seeds into dense groups.

Non-grass lawns

The idea of having a lawn using plants other than grass obviously appeals to many gardeners as I'm asked about it rather frequently. These plants must have the same characteristic of being able to create flat areas of greenery that are tolerant of being walked on and tolerate mowing or at least trim-ming. The most important among them are some of the carpeting species of thyme and *Dianthus* and the non-flowering variety of camomile called 'Treneague', but they shouldn't be considered as real alternatives to grass. None of them will tolerate the amount of wear and tear that grass turf can absorb. All of them look rather dismal in winter and will only thrive in the sun-niest situation and on light free-draining soil. All of them must be hand-weeded because, being broad-leaved plants themselves, they will be killed by selec-tive weedkillers. In the right position, they can be very pretty but I feel that you should consider them as small-scale features for large gardens rather than real substitutes for real lawns.

Stepping stones allow access across a lawn without creating a muddy mess

A GARDEN POOL

" The gentle babble of a fountain, a small waterfall or even the contented plop as goldfish break the water's surface bring an undeniable extra dimension to a garden. But although no garden is so small that space can't be found for some aquatic feature, gardens where small children play must remain pool-free until they are older. This very important constraint aside however, I am sure that any gardener who has once experienced the delight of water gardening will never choose to be without it again. "

Creating a water garden

The siting of a water garden is all-important. It must be sunny and, ideally, well clear of deciduous trees because autumn leaves are a pool's biggest enemy; they sink, decompose at the bottom and so deplete the water of oxygen while adding noxious and toxic gases. The site should also be level and if the overall garden has a slope, the pool is better at the top rather than the bottom unless you plan it as a semi-natural feature with a surrounding bog garden. Then the water running down the slope to overflow from the pool into the area around can be a positive advantage. The choice between such a semi-natural pool and a more formal and unashamedly artificial one should be made at the beginning of your planning. While there is nothing functionally difficult about having a formal pool in the centre of a rock garden or an informal one surrounded by an Italianate courtyard, you will inevitably discover that they look pretty odd.

Modern pools are most easily and reliably made from butyl rubber, a tough and flexible material that is very easy to lay. For a very small pool, a pre-formed glass-fibre liner is a possibility but these are generally obtrusively pale coloured inside, difficult to disguise and limit you, of course, to a pool of their predetermined shape.

Having chosen your site, mark out on the ground the shape of pool you require (use a hose pipe for curves) and then measure a rectangular area at least 50cm (1¾ft) beyond its limits to give you the size of rubber sheet that you will need. Dig the pool hole to a depth of at least 45cm (1½ft) and preferably 50cm (1¾ft); this depth is essential to enable your fish to survive the winter. Leave a ledge (or a series of ledges if the pool is large enough) around the margin to allow for planting those species that thrive in slightly shallower water. Finally, line the entire hole with about 5cm (2in) of sand; this is to provide a smooth surface on which to bed

ABOVE: A formal pool is most appropriate when surrounded by paving
BELOW: A semi-natural pool looks best well away from buildings

the rubber liner, for one jagged stone can cause a costly puncture.

Spread your rubber sheet over the hole, anchor it temporarily at the edges and then slowly fill the new pool with water. The rubber will stretch to fit the shaped hole as you do this. Finally, when the pool is full, provide permanent anchoring for the sheet at the edges; either with slabs for a formal pool or with more irregular stones and soil for a semi-natural one. Then allow about one month for the whole to settle down before introducing first plants and, after a further two weeks, fish.

Use plastic planting baskets filled with garden soil. Choose soil that has not been heavily fertilised and don't use any organic manures or composts. Place a layer of gravel over the surface of the soil as fish will stir it up and possibly dislodge the plants. In addition to those plants chosen for their attractiveness, you will also need submerged oxygenating plants, but in all plantings it is essential that you have the numbers and types of plant most appropriate to the dimensions of your pool. It is important too to introduce appropriate numbers of fish and also a population of snails. Select goldfish, golden orfe or shubunkins rather than such species as carp and tench, which will constantly stir up the mud.

Care of the pool

As with other herbaceous perennials, deciduous water plants should have the dead foliage and flower stems cut back in the autumn and, as with other perennials, they benefit from periodic division. It is my experience that water plants require no feeding, obtaining all

RECOMMENDED WATER PLANTS

Acorus calamus Sweet flag (marginal)
Alisma plantago-aquatica Water plantain (marginal)
Aponogeton distachyos Water hawthorn (water plant)
Azolla caroliniana Fairy fern (floating)
Calla palustris Bog arum (marginal)
Caltha palustris Marsh marigold, Kingcup (marginal)
Ceratophyllum demersum Hornwort (oxygenator)
Cyperus involucratus Umbrella sedge (marginal)
Elodea canadensis Canadian pondweed (oxygenator)
Hottonia palustris Water violet (water plant)
Hydrocharis morsus-ranae Frogbit (floating)
Iris Bog iris (marginal)
Lobelia cardinalis Cardinal flower (marginal)

Lysichiton Skunk cabbage (marginal)
Mentha aquatica Water mint (marginal)
Menyanthes trifoliata Bog-bean (marginal)
Myosotis palustris Water forget-me-not (marginal)
Myriophyllum verticillatum Water Milfoil (oxygenator)
Nymphaea Water lily (water plant)
Orontium aquaticum Golden club (marginal)
Pontederia cordata Pickerel weed (marginal)
Sagittaria sagittifolia Arrowhead (marginal)
Stratiotes aloides Water soldier (floating plant)
Veronica beccabunga Brooklime (marginal)

the nutrient necessary from the soil in which they grow. Purpose-made sachets of slow-release fertiliser are available for insertion into planting baskets and may well be of benefit but never under any circumstances should you use conventional garden fertiliser.

There are few pest and disease problems on water plants although aphids can be troublesome on some species but insecticides and fungicides should never be sprayed close to water. Blanket weed (green cotton-wool like growth) is almost unavoidable. The only realistic ways to control it are to pull it out physically or to use barley or lavender straw mats in the water (obtainable from specialist aquatic nurseries).

Water lilies and other aquatic plants are best planted in baskets

MAKING THE MOST OF A GREENHOUSE

" A recent survey revealed that a greenhouse was at the top of most gardeners' wants. It's almost certainly the largest single gardening purchase that anyone is likely to make, but very often the selection of size and type of structure is done with too little planning and still far too frequently I see greenhouses that are not being used in the most efficient manner. With a little forethought you can ensure that your greenhouse provides you with a range of options. "

Selecting your greenhouse type

There are merits and disadvantages in both of the most commonly seen forms of free-standing greenhouse: 'the glass to ground' pattern, usually with slightly sloping sides, and the older style with walls that are solid below staging level. The former generally have aluminium frames, the latter almost invariably wooden. My preference lies with the latter, partly because of the merits of wood but also because of the reduced heat loss through the solid side walls and the greater ease with which use can be made of the entire floor area.

A lean-to greenhouse is in effect, half of a free-standing structure and is especially valuable in a small garden.

A lean-to greenhouse is ideal in limited space

It utilises some of the warmth from the adjoining wall and makes good use of ground area. It's only really effective, however, against a sunny, sheltered wall and even then the vertical inner wall should be painted white to reflect as much light as possible.

What size to choose

The most popular size of garden greenhouse for many years was 1.8 x 2.4m (6 x 8ft) but more recently the 3 x 2.5m (10 x 8ft) house has gained greater favour and this is the size that I recommend. Although it offers 66 per cent greater floor area, the purchase price per square metre is less and the winter heating costs are only about 25 per cent higher. Ideally, a glazed or even a heavy duty plastic sheet partition should be erected within to divide the greenhouse into two equal compartments.

Where to put it

Few of us have a completely ideal site but it should be as close as possible to mains electricity and water supplies, in a level, open yet sheltered position, away from trees (especially deciduous trees) and of proportions such that the greenhouse can be orientated with its long axis east-west for the most uniform illumination. Every greenhouse should be firmly anchored and preferably erected on 20cm (8in) deep concrete foundations. Easily the best floor for a greenhouse is gravel over firmed soil; this allows water to drain away freely and an annual treatment with a garden disinfectant will eliminate any pests, disease organisms or weeds.

Heating and cooling

Even with insulation, a greenhouse with no artificial heat supply (generally called a cold greenhouse) will probably not be frost-free in many winters. By far the simplest and most easily regulated heating system is a thermostatically controlled electric fan heater, operated most efficiently if it is set to maintain a minimum of 7°C (40°F).

Every greenhouse should have double-skin bubble polythene film erected in winter which will cut down heat loss by about 40 per cent while in summer, you will need to limit heat gain with shade paint. But you must also have adequate ventilation: the total area of opening vents should be at least 15 per cent of the greenhouse floor area. Automatic vents that operate on an expansion principle are very useful when you can't attend to the greenhouse during the daytime.

Watering

The ring-culture system that I advocate for growing tomatoes (page 64) avoids major problems with watering summer crop plants. For watering plants in pots on the bench, most gardeners will probably be content to rely on a watering can. Capillary matting is only really effective when all pots are of the same size and it generally works more satisfactorily with clay than plastic pots for these make better contact with the mat. The water absorbent mat itself must be laid in a tray on top of the staging and is linked via a short wick to a reservoir of water. Several more or less automated watering systems are becoming available for garden greenhouses but they are often very fiddling to assemble and commonly suffer from nozzle blockages when algae grow on any liquid fertiliser that splashes to contaminate them.

How best to use your greenhouse

Most gardeners use their greenhouse for raising tomatoes during the summer months and as most families require about six plants, a 1.8 x 2.5m (6 x 8ft) structure will be almost fully occupied from spring until autumn, permitting no room for raising seedlings in the spring or taking cuttings. But with the larger greenhouse subdivided, one compartment (the outer one) may be used to accommodate the six tomato plants (three down each side). After these summer crops have been removed, the same compartment can provide sheltered frost-free space for overwintering fairly hardy plants such as fuchsias or for raising winter salads (aided if necessary by installing movable staging for the winter only). The second (inner) compartment contains permanent staging (including a small, heated propagator) and the greenhouse heating source and is used for overwintering more tender subjects such as

pelargoniums and for early and late season plant raising. After the removal of the summer crops the whole interior should be cleared and disinfected.

ABOVE: **A span greenhouse is best for most garden uses**
BELOW: **Make optimum use of greenhouse space with staging**

CONTAINER GARDENING

❝ *Growing plants in containers is as old as gardening itself but I don't think it has ever been more popular. Partly this is because of the huge array of container types now available, often at very little cost, but also because of the tremendous versatility that it offers. There is no garden, large or small, in which some containers can't be used to advantage and for new-comers to gardening, this method of growing offers an ideal way to try out some of your skills; mistakes are soon remedied.* ❞

Long- and short-term container plants

I find it useful to consider container gardening in these two categories because the materials and plants involved are rather different. Short-term containers are those in which plants with a relatively short display period are used: summer bedding plants, bulbs, herbs, even vegetables if you wish. Long-term containers are those with more or less permanent plants: shrubs, large clumps of orna-mental perennials, small ornamental and even fruit trees.

Short-term containers

All containers must have drainage holes and be filled with good quality compost. I now use soil-based John Innes No 2 Potting Compost for most of my short-term plantings with the exception of hanging baskets. For short-term plantings, I don't advise using any container less than about 20cm (8in) in diameter because with the heat of the summer and plants that are generally shallow-rooted, a container smaller than this will dry out disproportionately quickly. Window boxes are rather different, however, for the trick here is to use as attractive a box as you can afford, provide drainage holes, line it with plastic sheet (also of course with drainage holes), and then place smaller

pots containing your plants within. In all cases, begin adding a proprietary liquid fertiliser to the water after about six weeks.

Any short-term container should be planted up using your largest plant or plants in the centre with smaller ones around it, finishing with trailing types to tumble over the sides. Among bedding plants, of course, there are the reliable stand-by species: petunias (including the trailing 'Surfinia' varieties), lobelias

A small tree can be grown in a container to enhance a paved area

Bulbs are perhaps the ideal container plants

(both cascading and bush types), helichrysum, impatiens, fibrous rooted begonias, thunbergia, schizanthus, verbena, nepeta, nasturtium and so on. But you can be much more imaginative and use lysimachia (creeping jenny), brachyscome (Swan river daisy), diascia, irisine, bidens, scaevola, bacopa and also lantana which looks a delight with its flowers of varying colours. You will find most of these at your garden centre.

For a herb container, the more obvious candidates are compact 'Curlina' parsley, creeping thymes, variegated sage, creeping pennyroyal mint, chives and golden marjoram. Bulbs are obvious container candidates and the greatest impact is achieved with successions of bulbs. You can achieve this most effectively by selecting plants with different flowering times and planting them in alternate rows and at varying levels (page 43).

Long-term containers

The choice of containers for semi-permanent plantings will almost certainly be dictated ultimately by cost but I would always urge you to buy the best and most attractive that you can afford. The best value among really big containers are undoubtedly wooden half-barrels which should be lined with plastic sheet (with holes for drainage), in order to keep compost and wood out of contact with each other. Having chosen your container and positioned it (yes, do this first, empty), you need a good quality compost and here there can be no compromise. The compost for a long-term planting must be soil-based John Innes No 3 Potting Compost.

I have said many times that any plant can be grown in a container. Shrubs of most types are reliable but do bear in mind that deciduous varieties will look uncompromisingly bare once they have shed their leaves. Evergreens, by contrast, can be placed in sheltered spots to protect them from the ravages of winter. Trees make surprisingly good container subjects provided you are careful to check on their ultimate size.

Using containers in your garden

Let's now see how containers can fit into the garden as a whole. Hard areas are both a blessing and a curse to a gardener; you simply can't put plants where you wish and you can't smash holes in paths and paving to create planting positions. It is here that containers come to the rescue and provide so much versatility for they mean that a choice plant can be put anywhere. So a focal point in a paved courtyard can be produced instantly, and a feature can be created to brighten up and add interest to a dark corner. And, against a wall, by using a container, a climber can be used to clothe a surface that otherwise would have to remain bare and boring. And that, after all, is the very essence of all container gardening.

A small trough enables you to grow alpines in a limited space

LEAFY SALADS

" Of all the crops that are best eaten fresh from the garden, those that I call 'leafy salads' must top the list. There is quite frankly no lettuce like the lettuce that 10 minutes earlier was growing in your own soil; and they are pretty easy to grow too. Unlike true vegetables, they are usually eaten raw (although some make good soups), often as an accompaniment to a meal rather than forming a major component, but in case anyone thinks that leafy salads begin and end with lettuce, read on; and then grow some. "

Lamb's lettuce

Rocket

Soil and site

Leafy salads require good growing conditions; on poor or under-fertilised soil or in shade, they will be at best tasteless and at worst, bitter. All suffer, however, to some degree from a site-related problem: in common with certain vegetables, they will run to flower and seed ('bolt'), and they will do so especially in hot, dry conditions and on light soils. The ideal soil, therefore, as for most vegetables, is a moist but free-draining, fairly rich neutral loam.

Individual crops

Endive: like lettuce but hardier, some types must be blanched to remove bitter taste. This is done by placing an unturned plant pot (with the hole sealed to exclude light) over them. Sow at intervals from Spring to Autumn and thin to 20 x 20cm (8 x 8in). Crop is ready in about 15-20 weeks. *Recommended varieties:* 'Batavian Broad-Leaved' (broad leaves).

A selection of different leafed lettuce varieties can look stunning

Lettuce: a multiplicity of new varieties means that lettuce has never been more popular. Sow at intervals from early spring to late summer (by careful choice of varieties and by using a greenhouse and cloches, it's possible to have year-round crops, but this takes rather precise planning). The most reliable results (especially early in the season) come from transplanting pot-grown plants raised from seed in a greenhouse or cold frame. Be sure to distinguish between hearting lettuce (butterhead, crisphead or cos) which are harvested in one fell swoop, and leaf lettuce that remain in the ground as 'cut and come again' plants. Space at 15 x 15cm (6 x 6in) to 25 x 25cm (10 x 10in) depending on the size of the plants. Crop is ready in about 6-15 weeks. *Recommended varieties:* 'Tom Thumb' (small butterhead); 'Webb's Wonderful' (crisphead); 'Little Gem' (small cos); 'Salad Bowl' and 'Red Salad Bowl' (leaf lettuce – pull away leaves as needed).

Rocket (or roquette if you are in a fashionable restaurant): this is a plant that has been rediscovered by chefs in recent years although it's been grown in gardens for centuries. It has a spicy, rather hot flavour. Sow it in succession in spring and early summer, and then replace it with land cress (see below). Space at about 7 x 7cm (2¾ x 2¾in). Crop is ready in about 6 weeks. There are no named varieties.

Land cress: use it similarly to rocket, or as a substitute for water-cress as it has a hot taste. It's a hardy crop and the best leafy salad to grow outdoors over the winter. Sow from spring to early

Leaf, oakleaf, butterhead, cos and crisp are the main lettuce types

summer and then again in late summer at a spacing of about 15 x 10cm (6 x 4in). Crop is ready in about 6 weeks. There are no named varieties.

Corn salad: also called lamb's lettuce, this is not quite as hardy as land cress and is also prone to rot in wet conditions but is also a particularly good winter crop. It has a less spicy, and more of a nutty flavour. Sow during the spring and again during the autumn at a spacing of approximately 15 x 10cm (6 x 4in). Crop is ready in about 8 weeks. There are no named varieties.

57

LEAFY VEGETABLES

" Generations of children have grow up trying to avoid most of the plants on these pages; and countless parents have spent their time telling them how much goodness they are missing. It's no use me trying to convince you that there's much glamour about these crops, but most are fairly easy to grow provided you have room, as most are also fairly big. "

Soil and site

The conditions must be very good to grow these plants well. The soil should ideally be a rich, moist but free-draining loam with plenty of organic matter dug in annually. Add generous applications of fertiliser before planting and during the growing of the crops, as leafy growth requires plenty of nitrogen.

Individual crops

Brassicas: this is the name given to edible plants of the cabbage family: most importantly cabbage itself (including red cabbage and spring greens), winter cabbage or savoy, Brussels sprouts, broccoli (purple-sprouting), calabrese (or annual broccoli), cauliflower and kale. It is the flowerheads rather than the leaves that are most important with cauliflower and the broccolis, they fit in to this group as far as cultivation is concerned. They are all (with the exception of non-hearting spring greens) best sown in a seed bed or in pots (important with cauliflower which is intolerant of root disturbance) for transplanting when six weeks old. Individual differences are as follows:

Broccoli: sow in late spring, space at 30 x 30cm (1 x 1ft). Crop is ready in about 12 weeks (calabrese) or 40–45 weeks (sprouting broccoli). Pick individual spears.

Recommended varieties: 'Corvet' F1 (calabrese); 'Purple Sprouting Early' (sprouting).

Brussels sprouts: sow in late spring, space at 90 x 90cm (3 x 3ft) for normal picking or 50 x 50cm (1¾ x 1¾ft) with an F1 variety for a crop of small buttons for freezing. Crop is ready in 27-36 weeks when the buttons are firm.
Recommended varieties: 'Cambridge No. 5', 'Fortress' F1; 'Peer Gynt' F1.

Spring cabbage or 'spring greens' are welcome after the winter

Perennial spinach doesn't run to seed in the way that true spinach does

Purple sprouting broccoli deserves a comeback in the kitchen garden

Cabbage/savoy: sow in summer for spring cabbages, early spring to late spring for summer and autumn cabbages, late spring for winter cabbages. Space at 30 x 30cm (1 x 1ft) (spring), 35 x 35cm (1¼ x 1¼ft) (summer, autumn and winter); 15 x 15cm (6 x 6in) for non-hearting greens. Crop is ready in 20–35 weeks, once heads are hard.
Recommended varieties: 'Hispi' F1 (spring); 'Golden Acre' (summer); 'Christmas Drumhead' (autumn); 'Ruby Ball' (red).

Cauliflower: sow in spring in pots (see above). Space at 50 x 50cm (1¾ x 1¾ft) (summer varieties), 60 x 60cm (2 x 2ft) (autumn and winter varieties). Crop is ready in 18–25 weeks (summer and autumn varieties), 40–50 weeks (winter varieties).

Recommended varieties: 'Dok Elgon' (summer/autumn); 'Walcheren Winter 1 Armado April' (spring - strictly these so-called 'winter cauliflowers' are spring broccoli)).

Kale: sow in late spring (earlier for curled varieties). Space at 45 x 45cm (1½ x 1½ft). Crop is ready in 30-35 weeks.
Recommended varieties: 'Pentland Brig'.

Celery: there are two types of celery. Trenched is hardy, and has much the better flavour but is difficult to grow, while self-blanching is easier, non-hardy and by and large tasteless. Both need a rich, moist soil. For trenched celery you must prepare a trench in the spring, approximately 40cm (1¼ft) wide and 30cm (1ft) deep, with a layer of well decayed compost or manure in the bottom. Sow in pots in spring, plant out after the last frost. Space at 20 x 20cm (8 x 8in) for self-blanching types, 20cm (8in) apart in the trench for trenched varieties. When trenched varieties are about 30cm (1ft) tall, fill the trench with soil and continue to draw soil around the plants to create a ridge, so that only the tops of the plants show. Crop is ready in 25 weeks for self-blanching types or 40 weeks for trenching types. *Recommended varieties:* 'Giant White' (trenched); 'Golden Self Blanching 3' (self-blanching).

Spinach: a hugely under-valued vegetable but difficult on light soils and in dry weather as it bolts (runs to seed). If this is a persistent problem, grow leaf beet (perennial spinach) (page 58) instead. Sow in growing position at intervals from early to late spring. Space at 25 x 15cm (10 x 6in). Crop is ready in 8–15 weeks. *Recommended varieties:* 'Longstanding Round'.

Celery takes rather a lot of effort but the results can be rewarding

59

THE ONION FAMILY

If you are thinking of growing anything for the kitchen, onions must be close to the top of your list of essential crops. Their strong and familiar flavours are vital ingredients in an enormous range of dishes, in traditional British as well as southern European and Asian cuisine. There is nothing particularly difficult about the cultivation of any of them and I have included here the familiar vegetable onions, salad onions, shallots and garlic, together with closely related plants that are generally planted in a herb garden but are conveniently considered here.

weeding must be done by hand; using a hoe will cause root damage.

Individual crops

Bulb onion: these are the large onions used for cooking. The two main types are the normal white skinned varieties

Soil and site

Onions won't tolerate a water-logged or heavy soil and they require plenty of sun for ripening and imparting a full flavour. They also benefit from a fairly high organic matter content in the soil.

General cultivation notes

There are certain general and rather unusual features about growing onions and their relatives. First, many types may be grown either from seed or from small bulbs called sets. Raising them from seed is cheaper but as these are all slow-growing plants and require a long season, a very early start is often needed, sometimes in pots in a green-house. Sets offer a much easier option because they can be planted directly outside later, when the soil is warmer and the crop will be given a flying start. They are also, of course, proportion-ately more expensive.

Onions have brittle or at least fragile roots; they resent disturbance. It's for this reason that sowing the seed in pots necessitates a little extra care when planting out the young crop. And it's also important to weed care-fully among the growing plants. Onions are poor competitors which means that weeds will soon swamp them, but

Onions are slow growing but very easy; and a must for the kitchen

Leeks are reliable through the hardest of winter weather

and the milder red-skinned varieties. When buying seed or sets, you must distinguish between those that are grown in the traditional way for summer harvest from spring planting or sowing, and the hardier, mainly Japanese varieties for autumn planting to provide an early crop the following year. Sow in growing positions, sequentially in spring; and then again in late summer (choose winter-hardy varieties for a spring crop). Alternatively, sow seeds in small pots or modules in a greenhouse in mid-winter for transplanting. Sow groups of four or six seeds together; this will result in medium-sized bulbs more suitable for kitchen use. Space at 25 x 10 cm (10 x 4 in). Crop is ready in 18–22 weeks (spring sown or planted), or up to 45 weeks (autumn sown or planted). *Recommended varieties:* 'Ailsa Craig'; 'Bedfordshire Champion'; 'Brunswick' (red); 'Senshyu Semi-Globe Yellow' (overwintering).

Salad (or spring) onion: varieties that are pulled green for eating raw; immature bulb onions may be used but specifically selected varieties are better. Sow in growing positions sequentially from early spring to summer and again in late summer (winter hardy varieties for a spring crop). Space at 15 x 1cm (6 x ½in). Crop is ready in 8–18 weeks. *Recommended varieties:* 'White Lisbon', 'White Lisbon Winter Hardy '.

Shallots: strongly flavoured small onions, usually grown from sets. Plant in early spring with tips just showing above soil, spacing 20 x 10 cm (8 x 4 in), crop is ready in about 18–20 weeks. *Recommended variety:* 'Golden Gourmet'.

Leek: non-bulbing mainly winter vegetable, relatively easy to grow. Sow in seed bed in spring for transplanting to growing positions when about 20cm (8in) tall. Trim the root and leaf tips before planting. Drop the transplants into holes 15cm (6in) deep and then fill the hole with water. Space at 30 x 15cm (1ft x 6in). Crop is ready in 30–45 weeks. *Recommended varieties:* 'King Richard' (early); 'Musselburgh' (winter).

Garlic: very strongly flavoured and very easy to grow. Plant individual cloves (from supermarket) in autumn, space at 25 x 15cm (10 x 6in). Crop ready in 30-35 weeks. No named varieties.

Chives: clump-forming, non-bulbing perennial herb. Plant plants or sow seed in spring, one plant will suffice, divide every few years. No named varieties.

Tree onion or Egyptian onion: perennial onion with small, shallot-like bulbs at the top of the stem, instead of flowers. Buy plants and divide every few years. Use bulbs, with their hot taste, like shallots.

Garlic will grow surprisingly well in most climates

ROOT VEGETABLES

❝ I've grouped together here a range of familiar and very important vegetables, not closely related to each other but all producing their main edible part below ground. They range from the commonplace, but much under-appreciated potato, to crops that, are far as many gardeners are concerned, are somewhat exotic, such as celeriac and kohl-rabi. ❞

thinning is necessary after emergence) space at 18 x 10cm (7 x 4in). Crop is ready after 11–16 weeks.
Recommended varieties: 'Boltardy'; 'Cheltenham Green Top'.

Soil and site

Although the underground parts of these crops differs (in some it's a tuber, in other a swollen root or base of the stem), they are all prone to attack by rot and decay if the soil becomes waterlogged. They need to grow without serious impedance, so the finer the soil structure, the better; a lumpy, stony soil will never yield the best results.

Individual crops

Beetroot: one of the easiest of the root crops because the root swells at the surface of the soil. Sow in sequence from spring to early summer (each 'seed' is a cluster of individuals, so

In limited space, early potatoes take priority over the main crop

There's no need to try to be self-sufficient with vegetables but do grow a few rows of each of your favourites

Carrot: must have good, free-draining rich soil. Sow sequentially from spring to summer, space at 15 x 6cm (6 x 2¼in). Crop is ready in 12–16 weeks. Recommended varieties: 'Fly Away' F1 (more or less all season, carrot fly resistant); 'Early French Frame' (early, spherical); 'Autumn King 2' (main crop to keep in ground over winter).

Kohl rabi: one of the most prized of vegetables in parts of central and eastern Europe. It is more closely related to the cabbage and the cauliflower than the turnip, which it superficially resembles. Sow sequentially from spring to summer, space at 30 x 15cm (1ft x 6in). Crop is ready in 8–12 weeks. *Recommended variety:* 'Purple Vienna'.

Swede: can be tricky as it tends to become hard and woody in many soils. Sow in late spring or early summer,

space at 30 x 20cm (1ft x 8 in). Crop is ready in about 20 weeks. *Recommended variety:* 'Marian'.

Turnip: like the swede, not easy to grow well unless the soil conditions are good. Sow in spring (early varieties) or summer (maincrop varieties), space at 20 x 10cm (8 x 4in) (early varieties) or 25 x 12cm (10 x 5in) (maincrop varieties). Crop is ready in about 6–12 weeks. *Recommended varieties:* 'Snowball'; 'Purple Top Milan'.

Parsnip: easier than carrots as more tolerant of poorer soils but much bigger plants. Sow in spring, space at 30 x 15cm (1ft x 6in). Crop is ready in 30–35 weeks. *Recommended varieties:* 'Avonresister'; 'Gladiator' F1.

Potato: an excellent crop to grow on new land as it improves soil structure and suppresses weeds although it takes up plenty of room. If space is limited, grow early varieties only. Buy tubers of early varieties in late winter to early spring and spread them out in trays to sprout in a warm, light place. Plant early varieties in mid-spring, maincrops in late spring. Space at 60 x 30cm (2 x 1ft) (early varieties), 75 x 35cm (2½ x 1¼ft) (maincrops). Crop is ready in 13 weeks (early varieties), 22 weeks (maincrops). *Recommended varieties:* Early: 'Charlotte'; 'Estima'; 'Rocket'; 'Sharpe's Express'; Maincrop: 'Desirée'; 'King Edward'; 'Pink Fir Apple'.

Radish: the easiest of all crops to grow but they must have water and sun to develop flavour. There are two main

types: the summer salad types and the less widely grown hardy winter radishes. Sow in sequence from early spring to early summer (summer types), and then in summer (winter types); space at 8 x 2–4cm (3¼ x 1¾–1½in) (summer varieties) or 15 x 15cm (6 x 6in) (winter varieties). Crop is ready in 3–6 weeks (summer varieties) or 9–12 weeks (winter varieties). *Recommended varieties:* Summer: 'French Breakfast'; 'Short Top Forcing'; Winter: 'Black Spanish Round'.

Jerusalem artichoke: a large relative of the sunflower, slow growing but tolerant of almost any soil and shade. Plant tubers from early to late spring, space at 1m x 50cm (3 x 1¼ft). Crop is ready in 45-50 weeks. *Recommended variety:* 'Fuseau' (smooth tubers).

Once you gain experience, try less common plants like kohl-rabi

Celeriac is a challenge to grow well if it isn't to taste woody

VEGETABLE FRUITS

Although the title of this section might sound totally illogical, in reality many of the most popular plants that we grow as vegetables are as much fruit as are apples, pears and raspberries. They are the seed producing parts of the plant and they have some things in common as far as cultivation is concerned. Peas and beans, which are no less the fruits of the plant, form a discrete group and I have described them on pages 66–7.

Soil and site

All of these crops originate in warm climates. They must, therefore, have sunshine and some of them (tomatoes, peppers and aubergines in many areas) must be grown in a greenhouse. They will generally be most successful in potting compost in some form of container: pots or growing bags are the most popular and convenient. Cucumbers (at least some varieties) and their relatives courgettes/marrows can be grown outside. All the crops require regular watering and most need regular applications of liquid fertiliser too.

Individual crops

Tomato: the most popular greenhouse crop although some varieties can be grown outside successfully most years in milder areas. Sow in 9cm (3½in) diameter pots approximately nine weeks before the plants are to be planted into their growing conditions, space two plants per standard sized growing bag, or 45cm (1½ft) apart in ring culture pots or greenhouse border soil; outdoors, 75 x 45cm (2½ x 1½ft), greenhouse and staked (cordon) outdoor varieties need canes for support and the side-shoots of these varieties must be pinched out regularly. Crop is ready in 16 weeks (greenhouse), 20 weeks (outdoors).

Recommended Varieties: Greenhouse and outdoors: 'Alicante', 'Gardener's Delight' (small fruit, very sweet taste), 'Sungold' F1 (small fruit, very like 'Gardener's Delight' but yellow), 'Yellow Perfection' (yellow fruit). Greenhouse only: 'Buffalo' (large fruited beefsteak type). Outdoors only: 'Incas' (Italian-style plum tomato); 'The Amateur', 'Red Alert', 'Sleaford Abundance' F1.

Sweet pepper (capsicum): grow in greenhouse but much lower growing than tomatoes and need no side-shooting or tall support, space three plants to a growing bag or 40cm (1½ft) between ring culture pots. Crop is ready in 18 weeks. *Recommended variety:* 'Salad Festival'.

Aubergine (egg plant): grow in greenhouse, space as pepper. Crop is ready in 20 weeks. *Recommended varieties:* 'Ova' F1. (white, spherical); 'Slice Rite' (purple).

Cucumber: tender crops for greenhouse or outdoors but the outdoor varieties grow and crop so quickly

You can obtain a crop of tomatoes even if your garden is paved over

into the compost, in 9cm (3½in) pots and remove the weaker seedling, plant into growing bags or pots of John Innes No. 2 compost in a greenhouse, or directly into a well manured planting position in a cold frame, space at 45cm (1½ft) in a frame or two plants per growing bag. Crop is ready in 12 weeks. *Recommended variety:* 'Sweetheart' F1.

Sweet corn: delicious when fresh but a small yield from such large plants. Tender and grown outside in summer. Sow seed individually in 9cm (3½in) pots and plant outside after last frost, space at 45 x 45cm (1½ x 1½ft). Crop is ready in 13 weeks. *Recommended varieties:* numerous very similar varieties are supplied by individual seed companies; there is nothing to choose between them.

A cold frame offers you the chance to grow less hardy crops like melons

(and taste so good) that I find the greenhouse space is wasted on them. Sow outdoors (with seed inserted sideways) in well manured planting position or in growing bag in greenhouse, space at 45 x 45cm (1½ x 1½ft) outdoors after last frost has or two plants per growing bag. Crop is ready in 8-10 weeks. *Recommended varieties:* Greenhouse: 'Petita' F1; Outdoor: 'Burpee's Tasty Green' F1.

Courgette (marrow): courgettes are immature marrows, always grown outdoors, like cucumbers in rich soil;

always choose bush varieties which take up much less room than trailing types. Sow seed in pairs, inserted sideways into the compost, in 9cm (3½in) pots and remove the weaker seedling, plant outside after last frost 60 x 60cm (2 x 2ft). Crop is ready in about 8 weeks. *Recommended varieties:* 'Gold Rush' F1; 'Zucchini' F1.

Melon: close relative of cucumber and courgette but not successful outdoors; best in a greenhouse or cold frame. Sow seed in pairs, inserting sideways

Courgettes are very easy; a bush variety will take up less space

PEAS AND BEANS

❝ The pea and bean family is one of the most important in any kitchen garden but some of the members take up very much more room than others and it's important to bear this in mind when planning your crops. In terms of yield, the approximate order of 'efficiency' is runner beans (the biggest crop from a given area), broad beans, French beans and finally peas, which, wonderful as they are when fresh, sadly aren't very practical for small gardens if you want anything approaching a worthwhile harvest. ❞

vegetables because bacteria on their roots produce small nodules which add nitrogen to the soil. For this reason, very little nitrogen fertiliser should be give to the crops as they may then produce lush foliage at the expense of flowers and pods.

Soil and site

A fairly moisture-retentive, but not waterlogged soil is ideal as these plants are very prone to root rotting. Most pea and bean crops (runner beans are the exception) will grow in slightly poorer conditions than other

Individual crops

Broad bean: a very hardy plant that offers the earliest bean crops in the spring. For these very early beans, however, you must choose the special over-wintering varieties. Sow in autumn (winter-hardy varieties only) or from early to mid-spring, space at 23 x 23cm (9 x 9in) for shorter varieties or 45 x 30cm (1½ x 1ft) for taller types. Crop is ready after 15 weeks (spring sown) or 25 weeks (autumn sown). *Recommended varieties:* 'Aquadulce Claudia' (early/overwintering); 'Imperial Green Longpod'; 'Red Epicure'.

French bean: these come in a very wide range of pod shapes and colours and, although most are low-growing plants, there are also some climbing varieties; all begin to crop before runner beans. Sow in mid-spring, space at 45 x 8cm (1½ft x 3¼in). Crop is ready after 8–13 weeks. *Recommended varieties:* 'Masai' (dwarf green pod); 'Purple Tepee' (dwarf purple pod); 'Corona d'Oro' (climbing yellow pod); 'Hunter' (climbing green pod).

Runner bean: probably the easiest and most highly rewarding of the group; often transplanted but I am convinced that sowing directly in to growing positions is better. The soil must be deeply

Runner beans can be attractive; this bicoloured variety is 'Painted Lady'

are those in which the young pod is eaten whole; and petit pois types, are those that produce very small peas even when mature. Sow in autumn and from early to late spring (according to variety), space in bands of three rows, 10cm (4in) apart, with 60cm (2ft) between the central row of adjoining triple rows; plants 10cm (4in) apart within the rows. Use twigs or netting for support. Crop is ready in 12-16 weeks.

Recommended varieties: 'Feltham First' (early); 'Kelvedon Wonder' (second early); 'Hurst Greenshaft' (maincrop); 'Sugar Ann' (sugar pod); 'Waverex' (petit pois).

LEFT: Dwarf beans come in a wide range of colours and pod shapes
BELOW: Add interest by growing a semi-leafless variety of pea

dug and manured. Canes or other supports are needed. Sow in late spring, space at 60 x 15cm (2ft x 6in). Crop is ready in 12 weeks.
Recommended varieties: 'Polestar' (stringless, red flowers); 'White Emergo' (string, white flowers); 'Painted Lady' (string, bicoloured); 'Hammonds Dwarf Scarlet' (dwarf).

Pea: home grown crops always have a far better flavour than any shop-bought produce, but a low yield per unit area and are rather prone to disease problems. It's important to distinguish the main types: round-seeded varieties are for autumn or early spring sowing to give the earliest crops; wrinkle-seeded types are for later sowing (divided into early, second early and maincrop varieties, by maturity); mangetout varieties

LONG-TERM VEGETABLES

" By its nature, the vegetable plot tends to be a constantly changing thing. Most vegetables are annuals or biennials grown as annuals, so it comes as something of a surprise to find a few that are the equivalent of herbaceous perennials. They remain in the same place for the whole of their lives, the edible parts being removed year by year. Although they are all quite unrelated to each other, they do often find themselves growing side by side, removed from the seasonal rotation, so it's appropriate for me to consider them together. "

Buy off-sets and plant in spring; every few years remove the off-sets from established plants to start afresh and discard the old stock. Space at 1 x 1m (3 x 3ft). Crop is ready for cutting after 18 months; cut the terminal flower first, then cut the others as they swell, but before the flowers open.

Individual crops

Rhubarb: although it will grow in most soils and is generally planted and then more or less forgotten, rhubarb is a crop that benefits greatly from a little care and attention so cover the crown with well rotted compost or manure in autumn. One plant should be sufficient for most needs and should be bought as a named plant, not raised from seed. Pull, rather than cut, the stalks as needed in spring and early summer.
Recommended variety: 'Timperley Early'.

Asparagus: sadly, asparagus isn't a plant for a small garden; the yield is just too low to justify the area needed. Buy one-year old crowns from a specialist nursery, plant in spring; prepare a trench 20cm (8in) deep and 30cm (1ft) wide, mound soil 8cm (3¼in) high in the centre and plant the crowns on this, then refill the trench, space at 30 x 30cm (1 x 1ft). Crop can be cut in early summer from second year after planting.
Recommended varieties: 'Connover's Colossal'; 'Lucullus'.

Globe artichoke: a huge relative of the thistle, the immature flower-heads are harvested to eat, but the yield is minute in relation to the size of the plant and the growing area needed.

For extra early, tender rhubarb, cover the plants to force them

ABOVE: Asparagus needs a fairly big area to give a worthwhile crop
RIGHT: Globe artichokes are big plants; and the yield is small

Recommended varieties: no named varieties normally available.

Seakale: a large but little known old garden vegetable, but unlike some outdated crops, one well worth growing. Can be raised from seed but better from root cuttings called thongs. Plant in late autumn, space at 45 x 45cm (1½ x 1½ft), remove flowering shoot to preserve the plant's energy. Force by covering the crowns in mid-winter, first with dry leaves and then with a bucket, upturned pot (with blocked drainage hole) or a traditional clay forcing pot. Stop cutting shoots in late spring.
Recommended varieties: no named varieties normally available.

HERBS

No garden is too small for herbs; and no kitchen can manage without them. Few are difficult to grow, few take up a great deal of room. But there is one fact with herbs that isn't widely enough appreciated and why many gardeners find their herb bed soon turns from being an attractive feature to a disappointment. Herbs are short-term plants; some are annuals and should be raised each season from seed but even the perennials require renewing every two or three years.

Soil and site

Most of our kitchen garden herbs originated in the Mediterranean and not surprisingly therefore, they benefit from a warm, sunny position and a light, free-draining soil. If your garden can't offer these conditions, then grow your herbs in containers of soil-based compost. But however you grow them, remember that kitchen herbs are of little value if they are a long way from the kitchen.

Individual crops

I have limited my selection here to herbs of culinary use. The huge range of herb plants that have been grown for medicinal or dyeing purposes form a fascinating subject in their own right but are outside my scope here. The only significant culinary types that I have excluded are the herb onions that I describe on pages 60–1.

Basil: a large range of colours and flavours is now available. Sow seed in spring, renew annually.
Recommended varieties: the commonest culinary variety is usually just called 'Sweet Basil' but all varieties are well worth growing.

Bay: the largest important herb plant; a tall evergreen bush or small tree.

Buy a plant and grow it as a perennial. *Recommended variety:* the normal species is used for culinary purposes.

Chervil: white-flowered hardy annual, raise from seed annually. No named varieties.

Coriander: similar to chervil although not quite as hardy. Raise annually from seed. No named varieties.

Dill: a tall yellow-flowered plant with very feathery foliage, similar to fennel. Raise annually from seed. No named varieties.

Fennel: similar to dill but perennial and hardier. Although perennial, the plants soon become very large and fennel is best grown as an annual or biennial. Self-seeds freely.
Recommended varieties: bronze form has attractive, olive green foliage but produces both green and bronze seedlings. A form with a swollen stem base is grown as a vegetable.

Horseradish: medium perennial with bright green and rather leathery leaves arising from a long, white tap root. Buy a plant but confine its roots with slabs or other means as it is very invasive and difficult to eradicate. No named varieties.

Marjoram/oregano: low-growing, clump-forming, slightly woody perennials with 60–80cm (2–2½ft) leafy stems arising annually from the base. Buy a plant and replace every two or three years or take shoot cuttings in late summer.
Recommended varieties: O. vulgare

A herb bed is a must; and can be pleasing to the eye

Horseradish must be confined in some way as it spreads wickedly

(oregano, common marjoram), the golden-leaved form 'Aureum' (gold marjoram) is especially attractive. *O. majorana* (sweet marjoram) also occurs in a range of varieties.

Mint: a large group of very strongly aromatic perennials. Mints, in general, are more tolerant than other herbs of shade and wet soil. Buy plants but confine them in pots (sunk in the ground) as they are invasive. Renew from pieces pulled off the plant every three years.
Recommended varieties: M. x *gracilis* (ginger mint); *M.* x *piperita* (black peppermint); *M. spicata* (spearmint); *M. suaveolens* and variegated form *M. s.* 'Variegata (apple mints); *M.* x *villosa alopecuroides* (Bowles' mint).

Parsley: a densely leafy biennial, best grown annually from seed, sowing in spring and again in autumn.
Recommended varieties: 'Moss Curled';

'Curlina' (a more compact form of the moss-curled type); 'Plain Leaved' (*P. crispum neapolitanum*), a taller plant 60cm (2ft) tall with flat, dark green leaves and a stronger flavour.

Rosemary: an evergreen bush; buy a plant and either keep it clipped or renew every few years as it becomes straggly.
Recommended varieties: several varieties exist with pink and white flowers as well as blues of varying intensities but for culinary use, the normal species is satisfactory.

Sage: a rather loose woody perennial, reaching approximately 60cm (2ft) in height. Buy a plant and renew every two or three years.
Recommended varieties: in addition to

the normal species, there are several attractive foliage variants.

Tarragon: herbaceous and not very hardy perennial with rather delicate upright shoots and soft, narrowly willow-like leaves. Buy a plant and renew every two or three years.
Recommended varieties: A. dracunculus is the true French tarragon with the best flavour.

Thyme: woody perennial, generally forming dwarf bushes although many forms are creeping. Buy a plant and renew every two years.
Recommended varieties: there are numerous varieties of several species, differing in overall habit, leaf colour and aroma. For culinary use, the most useful is *T. vulgaris* 'Silver Posie'.

Mint is another spreader but can be grown in sunken pots

SOFT FRUIT

> *The delicious taste of fresh vegetables notwithstanding, I do find that guests express greater appreciation at freshly picked soft fruit than almost anything else you are likely to offer them. The term 'soft' can be a bit puzzling as many other types of fruit, such as plums and cherries, turn pretty soft when they are ripe. In a gardening sense, however, it tends to be used for those fruits that are grown not on trees but on something smaller, generally a bush or clump of canes. The term 'soft fruit' therefore describes raspberries and related fruits, currants, gooseberries and strawberries.*

Site and soil

All types of soft fruit will thrive best in full sun and on a fairly well drained and moderately rich loamy soil. On drier, lighter soils, they will need regular applications of organic matter but on a heavy clay, they are unlikely to thrive. Apart, to a limited extent, from strawberries, soft fruit aren't easy subjects to grow in containers. In most parts of the country, however, you will always lose a fair amount of your crop unless you cover the plants with a cage as protection from birds. Most soft fruit (again, apart from strawberries) will crop effectively for at least seven years.

General cultivation

All soft fruit require additional fertiliser in the spring and they all require some pruning (see the notes on individual crops and also pages 84–7). The cane fruits and any fruits grown using the restricted training shapes called cordons require a set of horizontal support wires. A visit to a model garden or pick your own fruit farm will indicate to you how this is achieved. When obtaining new plants, always buy from a supplier offering certified virus-free stock. Don't propagate your own plants as the yield from plants affected by virus will be small and the cropping life short.

Individual crops

Blackcurrants: must be grown as bushes as they are not amenable to being cordon trained. Plant deeply, space at 1.2m (4ft), prune after picking or in winter, cutting back the oldest one-third of the shoots to just above the base.
Recommended variety: 'Ben Sarek'

Red and white currants: may be grown as bushes or cordons. Plant cordons in rows alongside support wires, space bushes at 1.8m (5¾ft), cordons at 30cm (1ft). Prune after midsummer and again mid-winter, cutting back main branches by one-third and side-shoots to just above five leaves from the base.
Recommended varieties: 'Red Lake' (red); 'Versailles Blanche' (white).

Gooseberries: may be grown as bushes or cordons. Plant cordons in rows alongside support wires, space bushes at 1.8m (5¾ft), cordons at 30cm (1ft). Prune after midsummer and again in mid-winter, exactly as red and white currants.
Recommended varieties: 'Careless' (early to mid-season); 'Invicta' (early to mid-season); 'Lord Derby' (late).

Raspberries: grow as canes in a row, spaced 70cm–1.2m (2½ –4ft) apart (depending on training system), prune immediately after fruiting (summer-fruiting varieties) by cutting out old fruited canes, or in late winter (autumn-fruiting varieties) by cutting all canes to soil level.
Recommended varieties: 'Glen Moy'

**ABOVE: In limited space, red currants are best grown as cordons
RIGHT: Raspberries should be pruned immediately after fruiting**

early, no prickles); 'Glen Prosen'
(mid-season); 'Malling Admiral' (late);
'Autumn Bliss' (autumn).

Blackberries and related fruits:
the blackberry is the cultivated bramble
but there are many related hybrid fruits
(most are crosses between blackberries
and raspberries), grow as canes in
a row, space at 2.5–4m (8–13 ft)
depending on vigour, prune by cutting
out old fruited canes after cropping
Recommended varieties: 'Loch Ness'
(early to mid-season, short upright
growth, thornless); 'Ashton Cross'
(mid-season, vigorous, probably the
best flavoured). Related hybrid crops
with large dark red or black fruits:
Boysenberry; Loganberry; Marionberry;
Tayberry; Tummelberry.

Strawberries: continually popular
but remember that as a garden crop,
they are short-term plants that take up
a good deal of room (they will yield two
or three crops at most and should be
rotated, like vegetables) and must be
protected from birds. Place straw or
other material beneath ripening fruit
to keep them clean. They can be grown
in containers but the yield is very small
and the whole operation time-consuming. Buy plants (preferably pot-grown
in degradable pots) and plant in autumn,
space at 30–45cm (1–1½ft) between
plants, 70–90cm (2½–3ft) between
rows. Recommended varieties:
'Aromel' (autumn, easily the best
'perpetual' strawberry); 'Cambridge
Favourite' (mid-season, the best all-
round variety); 'Pegasus' (late).

**RIGHT: Strawberries will crop earlier
if they are covered with fleece**

APPLES AND PEARS

❝ When a young friend moved some time ago to his first garden, already well established, he told me that the greatest pleasure and joy came in his experiencing, for the first time, the opportunity to pick an apple straight from the tree. It is a delight that he refers to still and it's something that those of us, like me, who were fortunate enough to grow up with apple trees, too readily take for granted. Today, with growth-limiting rootstocks and restricted training systems, there is scarcely any garden too small for its owners not to share in this satisfaction. ❞

Site and soil

Apples are the most versatile of all fruit trees and will grow in more marginal conditions than others. So although the best crops will always be obtained from that deep, rich, moist loam so beloved of gardeners, apple trees will fruit in most areas and in most soils. In small gardens, they are best grown as cordons or in containers; the growth limiting rootstocks now available mean that trees of almost any size can be pre-selected at the time of purchase. Simply choose your fruiting variety and order a tree that has been grafted onto the appropriate rootstock.

Pears are less adaptable than apples and must have better growing conditions and a warm position. They are not available on such limiting rootstocks and are difficult to grow in containers because of their size. They are nonetheless very amenable to training, especially as espaliers.

With few exceptions, it is important to grow more than one apple or pear tree of different varieties to facilitate cross-pollination. The nursery will advise you on the best 'partners' to select, as not all varieties will pollinate all others although a good rule of thumb is that varieties in flower at the same time will probably be satisfactory. One alternative option with apples is to buy a so-called 'family' tree in which more than one variety has been grafted onto the same rootstock.

Apples: when choosing trees, decide if the variety you want is a dessert or eating variety, a more acid-tasting culinary or cooking variety, or is dual purpose. Plant in late autumn (you will obtain the greatest choice of varieties by pre-ordering from a specialist fruit nursery who will send the trees, bare-rooted in the dormant season), space as shown in the chart, the tree will begin to crop in the first or second year after

A family apple tree has two or more varieties grafted together

EFFECTS OF GROWTH LIMITING APPLE ROOTSTOCKS

Rootstock	Height of free-standing tree after 10 years	Spacing		
		Free-standing	Cordon	Espalier
M.27	1.5m (5ft)	1.5m (5ft)	75cm (2½ft)	N/A
M.9	2m (6½ft)	3 m (10ft)	75cm (2½ft)	3m (10ft)
M.26	2.5m (8ft)	3.5m (11ft)	1m (3ft)	3.5m (11ft)
M.106	3–4m (10–13ft)	4.5m (14¾ft)	1m (3ft)	4m (13ft)
M.111	5m (16ft)	6m (20ft)	N/A	5m (16ft)

planting. Prune cordons and espaliers in summer and free-standing trees in winter. Only remove damaged branches from older trees. For further information on pruning and training, see pages 84–7 and my book *Best Pruning*. Recommended varieties: Dessert varieties (in order of maturing):

'Beauty of Bath'; 'Discovery'; 'Redsleeves'; 'Fortune'; 'James Grieve' (dual purpose); 'Greensleeves'; 'Ellison's Orange'; 'Sunset'; 'Blenheim Orange' (dual purpose); 'Jupiter' (triploid, requiring two other pollinators); 'Spartan'; 'Worcester Pearmain'; 'Crispin' (triploid, requiring two other

pollinators); 'Idared'; 'Tydeman's Late Orange'; 'Kent'; 'Golden Delicious'. Cooking varieties: 'Bramley's Seedling' (triploid, requiring two other pollinators); 'Howgate Wonder'.

Pears: more difficult to grow than apples, being slower to mature and less hardy. Your best chance of success is to grow a cordon or espalier against a warm wall. Rootstock's are limited, and most are grafted on to the moderately growth-limiting 'Quince C'. Plant in late autumn, space 1m (3ft) between cordons, 4m (13ft) between espaliers, and 4.5m (14¾ft) between free-standing trees; prune cordons or espaliers in summer and winter, free-standing trees in winter (see pages 84–7 and *Best Pruning*). Recommended varieties: 'Conference', 'Beurre Hardy', 'Williams Bon Chrétien', 'Doyenné du Comice'.

Cordon apples take up very little garden room

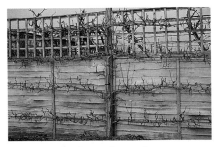

The espalier is perhaps the most stylish way to train fruit trees

PLUMS AND RELATED FRUIT

> *Although plums, damsons, cherries, peaches, nectarines and apricots are in the same family as apples and pears, they are grown and pruned rather differently, and conveniently form a distinct group sometimes called stone fruit. I think the commonest misconception about them is that some, at least, are relatively tender and unsuited to temperate gardens. In reality, the damson is probably the hardiest of all fruit while the factor limiting peach and nectarine growing is more likely to be disease than climate. Which leaves apricots, far hardier than most gardeners imagine and capable of being grown very successfully in many parts of the country.* 99

Site and soil

Most soils are suitable provided they aren't acidic (peaches, nectarines and apricots especially require some calcium in the soil) or markedly wet and cold. A sunny site is important for ripening the fruit and a sheltered one will lessen the likelihood of damage to the blossom from late frost. All of these trees are very suitable for training, ideally in a fan pattern, against a warm wall.

Cultivation notes

Plum, gage and damson: these are the easiest of the stone fruits for gardens as they can be grown as freestanding trees, in which form they take up a fair amount of room but require very little pruning. Most varieties are self-fertile so only one tree only is needed. Gages are small, usually green or yellow types of plum and slightly less hardy. Damsons are small plums and are hardier but the fruit is acidic. Plant in late autumn, space trees or fans 5m (16ft) apart if grafted on 'St Julien A' rootstock or 3m (10ft) if on 'Pixy' rootstock. Prune fan-trained plants in spring and summer. Established free-standing plums trees need little pruning but damaged growth should be cut out in spring not winter.

Suckers should be pulled out promptly. *Recommended varieties:* (all self-fertile).

Plums: 'Victoria' (mid-season, easily the best all round variety for dessert and culinary use); 'Marjorie's Seedling' (late); Gage: 'Oulin's Golden Gage'; Damson 'Merryweather'.

Peach and nectarine: fairly hardy, but the real limiting factor is leaf curl disease. Always best grown fan-trained against a wall. The nectarine is a smooth-skinned variety of peach and its requirements are identical. Plant in late autumn, space fan-trained plants on 'St Julien A' rootstock at 4m (13ft). Prune fan-trained plants in spring. *Recommended varieties:* Peach: 'Peregrine'; 'Rochester'; Nectarine: 'Lord Napier'

Apricot: hardier than peaches although earlier in blossoming so may need protection in early spring. Best when fan-trained against a warm wall. Plant in late autumn. Space fan-trained plants on 'St Julien A' rootstock at 4m (13ft). Prune established plants in spring and summer. *Recommended variety:* 'Moorpark'.

Sweet cherry: difficult to grow. There is only one self-fertile variety, they form large trees and birds take all the fruit. If you want to try, I suggest fan-training one against a warm wall. Plant in late autumn. Space fan-trained plants on the rootstock 'Colt' at 5m (16ft). Prune in spring and summer. Suckers should be pulled out promptly. *Recommended variety:* 'Stella'.

The plum family is ideally suited to fan training

ABOVE: Damsons are small relatives of plums and extremely hardy

Bitter cherry: a cooking cherry also known as the Morello, sour or acid cherry. Easier to grow than the sweet cherry, but also best when fan-trained, and successful even against a cool, shaded wall. Plant in late autumn. Space fan-trained plants on the rootstock 'Colt' at 4m (13ft). Prune in spring and summer. Suckers should be pulled out promptly.
Recommended variety: 'Morello'.

LEFT: Plums aren't available on truly dwarfing rootstocks

OTHER FRUIT

" If there is any aspect of gardening where gardeners, especially new-comers, are too conservative and too wary of experimenting, it must be in their choice of fruits. Apples, pears and plums are all excellent in their way but figs, grapevines and kiwi fruit, among others, require only a little more attention and are hardy enough to grow outdoors in many areas. "

Site and soil

All of these fruits will tolerate most soils to a reasonable degree, but, with the exception of figs, all will thrive best in a good, fairly rich and moist loam; most won't tolerate heavy clay (although cobnuts and filberts will do so moderately well) or water-logged conditions.

Individual fruits

Fig: will only reliably produce fruit if fan-trained against a warm, sheltered wall. They differ from other fruit trees in two respects: firstly, they must have poor soil and, secondly, the small embryo fruits formed towards the end of one season are those that mature and ripen the following year. Plant in spring, one plant will suffice on a wall at least 3m (10ft) wide and 2m (6½ft) high. Prune in spring.
Recommended variety: 'Brown Turkey'.

Grapevine: although fruiting outdoor vines are found in gardens, for a reliable crop I would always cultivate them in an unheated greenhouse. Plant in spring just outside the greenhouse then pass the main shoot in through a hole close to the base of the greenhouse wall. One plant will suffice. Prune established plants in winter and spring.
Recommended varieties: 'Black Hamburgh'; 'Siegerrebe' (white).

Figs are best trained against a warm wall; but are very vigorous

uniquely different: train as for a free-standing apple tree then, in late summer, use your hands to break all strong side-shoots growing from the main branches and leave them hanging. Cut the broken shoots back to 5–8cm (2–3¾in) in late winter or early spring.
Recommended varieties: Cobnut: 'Nottingham Cob'; Filbert: 'Kentish Cob'.

Walnut: only suitable for large gardens but I wish that more new gardeners would take a long-term perspective and plant a walnut tree. Plant in late autumn, one tree will suffice but unlikely to crop in under 10 years, don't prune mature trees. Normally sold as unnamed varieties.

Kiwi fruits are vigorous plants for larger gardens

For a good crop, grapes should be grown in a greenhouse or conservatory

Kiwi fruit: once known as the Chinese gooseberry, slightly hardier than the grapevine, and too vigorous for most greenhouses so grow it against a tall, warm wall. Plant in mid spring or early autumn, space at 6m (20ft) although female and male plants are often sold together in the same container for good pollination and should be treated as one plant for planting and spacing purposes but trained in opposite directions.
Recommended varieties: 'Hayward' (female); 'Tomuri' (male).

Mulberry: very easy to grow, very long lived and with a wonderful flavour. Plant in late autumn to winter except in cold areas when spring planting is safer, one tree will suffice, little or no pruning is required. Normally sold as unnamed varieties.

Cobnut and Filbert: suitable plants for wilder, wooded gardens as they need considerable room to grow with light shade and shelter, space at 5m (16ft), expect to harvest nuts after three or four years. Pruning is

WATERING

" Whereas watering your plants was once just another chore to be done, along with the weeding and pest control, it has now become an important subject in its own right. This is because water is a precious resource and we are increasingly having to pay for it pro rata. Careful consideration must, therefore, be given to how best to water the garden, when to do it and which plants benefit most. "

Improving the moisture retentiveness of the soil

If you live in a fairly dry part of the country or you have a soil that is light and free draining, you are likely to experience some drought problems in most years. Try, therefore, to improve the soil's moisture retentiveness by digging in organic matter regularly and by applying organic matter as a mulch in spring when the soil is already moist. Choosing plants that are naturally more drought tolerant will also help: species from the Mediterranean (such as many herbs) or South Africa (many summer annuals and tender perennials like pelargoniums) make good choices. Any plants with grey or silvery foliage are drought tolerant, the colour being due to numerous tiny hairs that restrict water loss from the leaf surface.

How much water and when?

Although all plants need water, you don't need to give it to them all of time. When water is in short supply or the weather is very hot, concentrate first on annuals, such as bedding plants and

Select a sprinkler that can be directed to where the water is really needed

A seeping hose will slowly trickle water among your plants

vegetables and then on fairly shallow-rooted perennials like rhododendrons and soft fruit. A good rule of thumb is to water them when they are beginning to mature: lettuces as they begin to heart up, potatoes at flowering time (when their tubers start to swell) and flowers as buds burst, for example. Plants in containers will always need regular watering: the smaller and more exposed the container, the more water it will need and hanging baskets may need watering twice a day in summer. But don't worry about your lawn; apart from newly sown or newly laid lawns or in conditions of extreme drought, lawns may turn horribly brown but will always recover. When possible, try to water plants in the evening as this gives the moisture a chance to soak into the soil surrounding the roots before the sun's heat causes it to evaporate.

Watering systems

The basic modern garden watering system comprises a hose-pipe (choose a double-wall, knitted type on a through-flow hose reel with snap-fit connectors), one good, adjustable sprayer that offers a gentle spray as well as a strong jet, and a comparable, adjustable pattern sprinkler. Take care to choose a sprinkler that will be appropriate to the size and shape of your garden.

Before using a sprinkler, always check with your local water company for any regulations or restrictions relating to their use. Remember that, by law, an outside tap used with a hose-pipe must be fitted with a back-flow prevention valve to avoid contamination of the water supply.

Watering in the greenhouse has its own particular problems and, if you intend doing a great deal of greenhouse gardening, then consider installing a

Direct water around the root area where it is most needed

trickle (or drip) irrigation system. Water, from the mains or from a reservoir, is carried along a series of narrow plastic tubes, each ending in a nozzle through which water drips. Each drip nozzle supplies one plant pot. These systems can be tricky to assemble and need time and patience to set up but, once established, are useful not only for greenhouses but for containers on patios or for hanging baskets. They also are very precise with water being directly delivered to each pot.

Capillary matting is also useful but much simpler: plant pots are set out on capillary matting contained in shallow metal trays, the matting being kept moist by contact with a water reservoir.

Conserving water

Rainwater can and should be stored whenever possible. One or more water butts can be positioned to collect water from buildings but only use this for outdoor plants in beds and borders, as the algal and fungal spores it contains may result in damage to greenhouse plants and seedlings. During periods of water restriction, domestic waste water from washing up bowls and baths should be used in the garden, although water containing bleach or chemical disinfectants or grease is best not used.

Types of water

The chlorine in tap water does not affect plant life, but soft water has very few mineral impurities whereas hard water contains large quantities of calcium or magnesium salts and can be damaging when used in containers.

FERTILISERS AND PLANT FEEDING

❝ *The use of fertilisers to feed plants is probably one of the aspects of gardening that beginners most tend to neglect. 'After all', I am sure the reasoning goes, 'I've never seen a plant die because it wasn't fed, and old Mr So-and-So's garden looks jolly pretty and he never feeds anything'. I can understand all these sentiments, but the chances are that old Mr-So-and-So has a cottage style of garden where everything has all but run wild. And no, your plants won't die for lack of food but if you want highly bred cultivated varieties (and especially cultivated fruit and vegetables), then without feeding, there's no doubt that they will be rather miserable specimens.* ❞

Difference between fertiliser and manures or composts

A compost or manure is used to improve the structure of the soil; it contains relatively little plant nutrient and you will need a very great deal to satisfy your plants' food requirements. Fertilisers are mixed chemicals of either artificial or natural origin that break down in the soil to release vital plant nutrients.

Fertiliser is best put alongside plants rather than thrown over them

Types of garden fertiliser

There is now a bewildering array of fertilisers, apparently blended for every possible type of plant and every possible circumstance. All that it is really important to understand, however, is that they contain, in varying amounts, three main ingredients: nitrogen (abbreviated to its chemical symbol N), phosphate (abbreviated to P) and potash (abbreviated to K). These three chemicals do different things: nitrogen is the most important and encourages leafy growth (the key to everything else), phosphate encourages roots to form and is valuable at planting time and potash stimulates flowering and fruiting.

You can mange to do all of your gardening pretty satisfactorily by having a short list of the following fertilisers:

1. A balanced general purpose solid fertiliser

This type is particularly valuable for use among vegetables and other plants at or just before the start of the growing season. The commonest artificial blend available in Britain is a granular mixture called Growmore. The principal organically based compound fertiliser is fish, blood and bone, a blend of dried blood, finely ground bone meal and sulphate of potash (not, of course, organic).

2. General purpose liquid fertiliser relatively high in potassium

A fertiliser of this type should be the mainstay of most gardeners' fertiliser usage during the height of the season. There are several branded liquid products of this type, including most proprietary tomato fertilisers.

3. Bone meal (organic) or superphosphate (artificial)

These slow-release sources of phosphorus should be used when planting trees, shrubs, herbaceous perennials and bulbs.

4. Two lawn fertilisers

Lawns should normally be fed twice a year, in spring and in autumn, but the nutrient requirements are different at these times and you should have two powder-formulated lawn fertilisers; one with a relatively high nitrogen content for spring and summer use and one relatively lower in nitrogen for autumn and winter application.

5. Rose fertiliser

Fertilisers formulated for roses contain a blend of the major nutrients but with special emphasis on potassium to encourage flowering. Although formulated specifically for roses, these fertilisers also provide an ideal balanced feed for other flowering shrubs.

How to apply fertilisers

Whether fertilisers are applied as liquids, granules or powders, it's important that they are spread as uniformly

Slow release fertiliser prolongs the effectiveness of potting compost

as possible in the area where they are needed. Powders and granules applied to individual plants or to rows of vegetables are almost always spread by hand and, with practice, you'll find it fairly easy to obtain even coverage. Modern fertiliser packet labels generally bear dosing instructions in grams per square metre (and sometimes in ounces per square yard too). Always remember to wear gloves and always wash your hands after handling any fertiliser.

For lawn fertilisers, use a small wheeled spreader for uniform dosing; these can often be hired from garden centres. On a small scale, liquid fertilisers can be applied by sprayer or, especially on a lawn, by watering can, but for large areas of garden, use a hose end dilutor; a container that can be fitted to the delivery end of a hose-pipe. The container is filled with a concentrated fertiliser solution and the flow of water through the hose draws out concentrate to deliver diluted liquid feed.

The hose-end dilutor easily delivers diluted liquid fertiliser

PRUNING

If only less experienced gardeners would free themselves from the notion that 'cutting back' is the same as 'pruning', I think they would find the task both more satisfying and more rewarding. 'Cutting back' suggests something far more drastic and severe and I would rather you thought of pruning simply as the removal of certain parts of plants in order to stimulate other parts to grow.

Principles of pruning

In the space that I have here, I can only outline the basic principles of pruning but these should be sufficient to enable you to tackle most garden plants with a fair degree of confidence. If you require further information about the specific needs of different plant, and especially of fruit trees which can be a little more complicated, then I refer you to my book *Best Pruning*.

Where to make pruning cuts

You should always make pruning cuts immediately above a bud, leaf, flower or branch division; never in the middle of a length of shoot. This ensures that natural healing of the cut surface takes place swiftly. Always make the cut approximately 5mm (¼in) above the bud or other growing part and sloping away from it. An important use of pruning is to control the direction of future growth and you can do this by looking at the way the buds face. By cutting above outward-facing buds you will encourage shoots to grow outwards, leaving a more open centre to your plant. By cutting above an upward facing bud, you will encourage shoots to grow upwards, giving a narrower, more upright habit overall, but with a greater likelihood of shoot

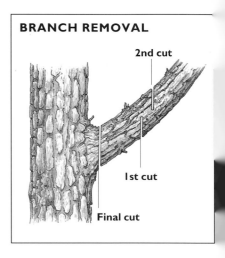

BRANCH REMOVAL

2nd cut

1st cut

Final cut

congestion in the centre. Take special care when removing large branches from trees, especially from the main trunk. Never allow the saw cut to damage the swollen base or collar of the branch, because it's within this zone that the tissues that promote healing are situated; and never apply wound sealing compounds to the cut surfaces of pruning cuts as this disturbs rather than aids the healing process.

When to prune

The easiest way to remember when to prune flowering and fruiting plants to achieve the best results is to relate pruning time to flowering time: in order not to remove flower buds, pruning is performed after flowering. But flowering and fruiting shrubs, trees and climbers fall into two groups: those that flower early in the year on wood that grew during the previous season (and therefore are pruned in spring) and those that flower after midsummer on wood produced during the current year (and which are pruned between late autumn and early spring). The first

Pruning cuts should be made above a bud and sloping away from it

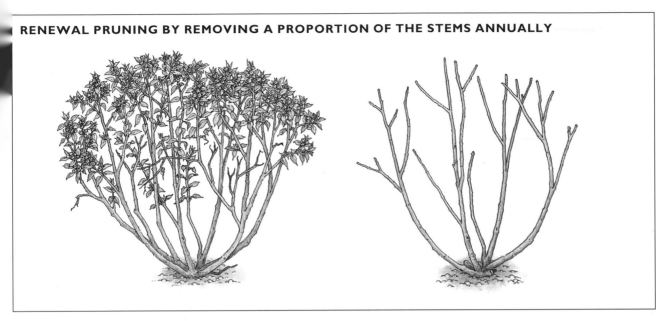

group is generally pruned very lightly (in other words, not much material is cut away, and the task is little more than a general tidying up and removal of dead flowerheads. The second group is generally pruned harder and not until spring so that the old growth provides protection in winter.

The timing of pruning for foliage plants is less critical but their ability to withstand frosts and cold winds needs to be taken into account. Any plant of borderline hardiness (and also many evergreens), are best pruned in the spring, although long growths that could be blown about and damaged in the wind may be removed in autumn.

How hard to prune

Other things being equal, the more growth that you remove from a plant, the more buds will in fact be stimulated to grow. The most important practical consequence is that severe (or as it is

Most shrub pruning should be done after the plant has flowered

Like many plants, cordon apples require both summer and winter pruning

usually called, hard) pruning should be used in order to encourage growth from a plant that is growing feebly or is inherently weak. Conversely, a very strongly growing plant should in general be pruned lightly in order to contain its vigour.

Types of pruning

SHRUBS

In order to try and keep things as simple as possible, I have chosen three categories that, together, account for most of the types of pruning that you are likely to need when tending to ornamental shrubs.

1. Renewal pruning of late flowering shrubs

This is a very important pruning technique for plants that flower after mid-summer. Either the whole plant is cut back to just above ground level in early spring, as with *Buddleia davidii*, autumn-fruiting raspberries and some dogwoods (*Cornus*); or, and more usually, only a proportion (usually the oldest one-third) of the stems is removed each season. The remaining stems are left unpruned or are lightly pruned (to less than one-half their length) and so the plant is entirely renewed every three years. This will maintain vigour and avoid the possibility of the plant becoming a congested mass of growth.

2. Light pruning of early-flowering shrubs

This is the commonest pruning technique for plants that flower before or shortly after midsummer. It is a more extensive version of dead-heading; the dead flower heads are cut back well beyond the base of the flowers and some re-shaping of the plant is done at the same time. Hand shears may be used to trim lightly over bushy plants as the flowers fade; trim to below the base of the dead flowerheads but no more than a few centimetres (about an inch) into the older wood.

3. Restorative pruning

You can often rejuvenate overgrown and neglected trees and shrubs by pruning out dead and diseased parts, overgrown and crossing branches and weak shoots, thus stimulating new young growth, although it is best to spread the task over three years, doing one-third of the pruning each year. Much of the benefit comes from allowing more light and air to penetrate the centre of the plant.

ORNAMENTAL TREES

Most ornamental garden trees need no pruning; the removal of occasional misplaced or broken branches should be all that is needed. If a tree needs to be pruned to limit its size, it has been planted in the wrong place. If, however, you have inherited an old, large and well established tree, I strongly advise you not to attempt any remedial work yourself. An expert will be able skillfully to reduce its height and overall size but it is a difficult and sometimes dangerous task.

CLIMBERS

Climbing plants are pruned using exactly the same principles as for shrubs. Clematis, which many gardeners find confusing, illustrate this well. They can be divided into three main groups for pruning purposes depending on when they flower:

Group 1 Clematis that flower early in the year on wood produced the previous season. Prune immediately after flowering by cutting back all weak and dead stems to just above a bud.

Group 2 Clematis that flower on wood from the previous season but in early summer; rather later than the Group 1 types. Prune in early spring by cutting out any dead or weak stems and cut back remaining shoots by about 30cm (1ft), cutting to just above a pair of plump buds.

Group 3 Clematis that flower later in the summer on the current year's wood. Prune hard in early spring to remove the previous season's growth, cutting back to just above a pair of plump buds about 75cm (2½ft) above soil level.

ROSES

Old varieties of shrub roses are pruned following the principles outlined for other shrubs. The two main groups of modern bush roses require rather more specific pruning in spring: for hybrid tea roses, prune back all shoots by half; for floribunda roses, prune back one-third of the shoots to soil level and prune back the remaining shoots by one-third.

FRUIT PLANTS

Full details of the pruning and training of fruit trees, bushes and canes are given in *Best Pruning* and I have insufficient space here to include all options. Most new gardeners will probably start with free-standing apple trees and their pruning is readily summarised.

In the first winter after planting, cut back the single shoot to a healthy bud at about 60–90cm (2–3ft) above soil level. This will result in several upright shoots being produced over the next year. The second winter, cut out the middle shoot to give the tree an open centre. The four strongest shoots remaining should be cut back by about half their length. Remember always cut to an outward-facing bud to maintain the open centre. Remove any other long shoots and cut back laterals to about three buds. In the third and subsequent winters, maintenance pruning takes over and the trees should be pruned in winter by cutting back the side-shoots on each branch to two or three buds above the base and shortening the leading shoots on each branch by up to one half. The less you need to cut back established trees, the better.

PRUNING TECHNIQUE FOR GROUP 3 CLEMATIS

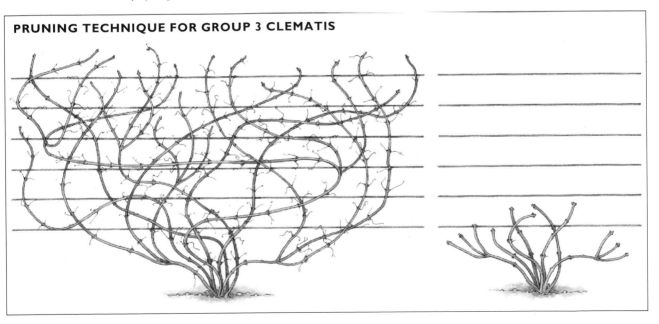

LAWN CARE

I indicated earlier in the book how important a lawn can be for a new gardener; either as a short-term expedient to help keep matters under control, or as a longer-term and very important garden feature. But no matter how much care and expense you put into buying and establishing your lawn, it will fail unless you give it a certain degree of annual attention and maintenance.

turf), I always believe you will obtain the best results if the mowings are removed and composted.

Always cut the edge of your lawn as well as mowing it, ideally with the edging shears that I described earlier

Mowing

Try to mow your lawn at least once a week during the main growing season. From autumn to spring, the amount of mowing needed will depend on the weather and the degree to which the grass has grown, but there's no reason why the lawn shouldn't be cut in mild periods during the winter too. Set the cutter blades to their highest at these times; cutting the grass short when frosts are still likely will result in death and browning of the grass leaves. During the summer, however, the blades can be lowered appreciably although it's unwise to cut grass at the lowest blade setting, for this merely encourages the growth of moss.

Although it's possible to mow with a side to side swinging action using a hover mower, I always prefer to mow in straight lines. This ensures that you cover everywhere uniformly and also helps if you want the lawn to have those very attractive stripes that are the result of using a cylinder mower but which can be produced by a rotary mower equipped with a small roller. For the finest effect of all, mow twice at right angles.

Although some gardeners advocate removing the grass collector from the mower in the cause of adding organic matter to the lawn (and there are even types of mower that deliberately thrust the chopped-up mowings back in the

A small electric scarifier will quickly remove moss and dead grass

(page 7). If time is really pressing and you don't have time to mow, you will find that trimming the edge of the lawn will itself immediately convey a neat and attractive appearance.

Scarifying

During the course of the summer, the turf of your lawn will inevitably accumulate a mass of dead grass, moss and weeds; material that is usually referred to as thatch. This will impede the free flow of rain, air and nutrients down to the roots and the grass will suffer in consequence. I can't stress too strongly the importance of a once a year (ideally in autumn) removal of this material. The operation is called scarifying and, although it can be achieved with a spring tine lawn rake, it is desperately hard work and buying or hiring a small powered scarifier makes sound sense. Always scarify after you have applied any autumn moss killer (see below). Initially the lawn will look like a hay meadow at harvest time but the material can be raked together for composting.

Feeding and weeding

Lawns must be fed and, as I indicated on page 82, two lawn fertilisers are needed, one for spring use and one for the autumn. I only use liquid, high-nitrogen 'green-up' feeds in the summer in years when very prolonged rain falls after the spring feed has been applied. I delay applying the spring feed until mid-to-late spring when the soil is really warm and moist; not so much for the benefit of the fertiliser itself but to ensure that the weedkiller that is

A daisy grubber can be used to remove individual weeds

combined with it is applied in conditions in which it's likely to be effective. Any weeds that do escape this treatment are dealt with later by localised application of a selective weedkiller in liquid form, either with a watering can (kept specially for the purpose) or with a weedkiller sprayer (although not with a hose-end dilutor).

Moss

The one lawn problem that causes gardeners more anguish and concern than any other is moss. There are gardeners who are obsessed with trying to rid their lawns of moss; and generally my advice is to expend their emotional and physical energies elsewhere. To kill moss isn't difficult. Any of the modern selective moss killers will do it, although none I think are better than the old remedy of lawn sand, but the moss will always return unless it's possible to correct the underlying causes. Moss will thrive when the grass is closely mown, when the lawn is shaded, poorly drained and the grass not fed.

A weedy lawn is very pretty but won't be as hard wearing

WEEDS

" I once knew an old gardener who was convinced that if he weeded his garden assiduously every year, a time would come when his plot would be weed free and he would be spared one of gardening's most irksome tasks. He was wrong, of course, although it is perfectly possible to limit most new weed growth to weeds whose seeds are blown in from beyond your boundary. But you need a combined strategy; and you really can't afford to relax. "

Why control weeds

Weed is simply the gardener's name for a wild plant but, because weeds are native species and a great many garden plants are not, they will generally be better equipped to grow in our climate and our soils. Ignore weeding and your garden plants will disappear, choked to death and starved of life's essentials.

Types of weed

Although there are a great many individual weed species in our gardens, you certainly don't need to be able to identify them all (although being able to tell the difference between a weed and a garden plant is very useful). It is, however, important to be able to recognise whether a particular weed is an annual or a perennial because this dictates how you can control it. The majority of the small weeds that spring up among vegetables and other growing plants are annuals. Groundsel, chickweed and shepherd's purse are familiar examples. By contrast, perennial weeds tend to be more important in places where the soil remains undisturbed for longer: on lawns, paths and among perennial garden plants. Thistles, ground elder, bindweed and dandelions are among the most common perennial weeds.

Controlling weeds

The most straightforward means of controlling annual weeds (or shallow-rooted perennial weeds, like daisies) is by digging or pulling them up or by cutting them down. Use your hands and a weeding fork for the former and a Dutch hoe for the latter and this can be done at almost any time of year although hoeing should only be performed if the weather is warm and dry so that the uprooted weeds will shrivel quickly. Hoeing and digging are, in a sense, curative methods of annual weed control; but how much better it would be if we could prevent weeds from emerging in the first place.

Much the simplest way to do this is with an organic mulch such as compost, leaf mould, well rotted manure or shredded bark laid on the soil surface. A layer about 5cm (2in) thick will prevent most annual weed seedlings from reaching the surface. An alternative to an organic mulch for weed control is opaque plastic sheet but it really isn't very pretty.

The purely physical approach is of much less value with persistent perennial weeds, principally because of the near impossibility of removing every fragment of root and rhizome and because of the plants' abilities to regenerate from the pieces left behind. Nonetheless, when clearing a new area of land, especially on a light soil, I have many times proved that it is perfectly possible to eradicate couch grass, nettles, thistles, and several other types of perennial weed by regular digging although I doubt if the extremely far-reaching weeds, such as bindweed or ground elder, can ever

Ground elder may be treated with a translocated weedkiller

Horsetail is one of the most difficult common garden weeds to control

be cleared totally in this way. Inevitably, therefore, most gardeners, at some time, will need to use a weedkiller, especially to control perennial weeds. There are basically two very important groups of weedkillers: total weedkillers kill all vegetation, while selective weedkillers only kill certain types of plant and the most important are those that kill only broad-leaved weeds and can therefore be used safely on lawns. Some weedkillers kill green tissues by contact; others are absorbed and then translocated (moved) within the plant, and these are of special value for deep-rooted persistent perennial weeds. Weedkillers that contain the chemical glyphosate are very important members of this group.

Residual weedkillers (which are also usually total weedkillers) persist in the soil for some time to kill seeds or freshly germinated seedlings. Clearly, a residual total weedkiller will clear an area of plant life for some time

(even for a season or more) so such a product should only be used on paths or other unplanted areas. Non-residual total weedkillers kill all existing vegetation but are rendered inactive in the soil, so replanting or sowing can proceed very soon afterwards. When

controlling weeds with weedkillers, it's generally more important to take account of where the weeds are growing than of what species they are. Don't be afraid of using weedkillers but, in all cases, read the label directions very carefully.

Goose grass is an annual weed and is easily removed by hand

PESTS, DISEASES AND DISORDERS

" *All living things have enemies among other living things. Plants are no exception and you won't garden for very long before you discover spots on leaves, pieces missing from flowers or even entire plants keeling over to die in circumstances of abject misery. Fungi, bacteria and viruses are the causes of plant diseases, while almost every known subdivision of the animal kingdom can offer a contribution to the roll call of pests. You can't control them all: the totally healthy garden is a biological impossibility and you shouldn't even attempt to create it, nor should you try to emulate commercial plant growers with their goal of blemish-free produce. Be extremely selective and learn, as much through experience as anything, where intervention is needed and where it isn't.* "

Prevention

Always buy plants and planting material from reputable suppliers in the expectation that it will be healthy, and always reject any that are obviously malformed or blemished or bear signs of pests. Much prevention can also be achieved through what I call garden hygiene. A neat and tidy garden is much more likely to be healthy than one that is cluttered with rubbish, debris and the remains of old plants. Rubbish creates hiding places for pests such as woodlice and snails, and as some fungi can live equally effectively on dead and living plant material, they can spread from debris to attack living plants.

Identification of problems

Inexperienced gardeners have two main concerns about pests and diseases: first, that of distinguishing between what is a problem and what is normal and to be expected. There

Sap-sucking aphids will soon weaken plants if they aren't controlled

are unfortunately no simple rules here and I refer you to my book *Best Garden Doctor* for identification charts. But second, and even more importantly, having recognised a problem, of knowing if and when they need to do anything about it. Here common sense will go a long way. If the yield of a crop or the impact of an ornamental is seriously being reduced (by an infestation of caterpillars for example), then some remedy may well be called for. If the effects (like scab on apples) are merely disfiguring, tolerance should be exercised.

Treatment of problems

Physical traps and barriers
These can be extremely useful for controlling some pests in the garden. At their simplest, these traps can be sticky cards to enmesh whitefly while at their most advanced, they can be pheromone baited devices to lure and ensnare male fruit moths. Barriers too can range from fencing to keep out deer or rabbits to netting over or around soft fruit in order to keep out birds, or from lightweight fleece over vegetables, protecting them from egg-laying flies or caterpillars to prickly twigs around soft plants to deter slugs.

Biological controls
Recently, several methods (called biological controls) have been perfected whereby natural parasites and predators can be used in the control of pests (there are no biological control methods to use against plant diseases),

Leaf spotting is often more disfiguring than really damaging

It's important to understand that not all fungicides or insecticides control all types of disease or pest with equal efficiency, so do read labels very carefully. Unless you have one specific or unusual affliction, try to buy those products that will treat a wide range of problems: many proprietary rose treatments for instance include a fungicide to control mildew, black spot and rust, while also containing an insecticide to combat aphids.

Safe use of garden chemicals
Read the label carefully and use the product only in the way and for the purpose described.

Don't use any chemicals that have lost their labels and don't decant chemicals from a large pack into a smaller one. Garden chemicals must only be kept in their original packaging.

Don't mix or prepare garden chemicals in the kitchen, and keep sprayers, watering cans or other equipment specifically for pest and disease control. Don't use the same equipment for fertilisers and weedkillers.

Wash out equipment thoroughly after use and pour excess diluted product on to an area of waste ground. Waste concentrated products should be disposed of according to the advice offered by your local authority.

Store all chemicals out of reach of children and pets, preferably in a locked cupboard and away from extremes of temperature.

Don't spray plants in strong wind, in bright sunlight or when flowers are fully open. The best time is in the early morning or late evening when bees are fairly inactive.

mainly in greenhouses but increasingly outdoors too. Some are on sale at garden centres but several only by mail order.

Chemical remedies
In garden centres or garden shops, you will see a very large display of chemicals on sale. How do you make a choice?

Iron deficiency is a common symptom on chalky soils

INDEX

PHOTOGRAPHIC ACKNOWLEDGMENTS

Professor Stefan Buczacki 5 top left, 33, 52, 93 top, 93 bottom

Garden Picture Library/John Glover 9, 63 left, /Jacqui Hurst 59 bottom,
61 top, /Lamontagne 5 bottom right, /Howard Rice 56 top right
John Glover 79 bottom right

Octopus Publishing Group Ltd. /Andrew Lawson front cover right, front
cover background, endpapers, /Howard Rice, front cover left, back cover, 1,
2 top left, 2–3 background, 7 left, 7 right, 13, 15, 19 left, 19 right, 21 top,
21 bottom, 22 left , 22 right, 23, 24 left, 24 right, 25, 26, 27 left, 27 right, 28,
29 top, 30 left, 30 right, 31 left, 31 bottom right, 32 top right, 32 bottom left, 34
left, 35 right, 35 top left, 36 top right, 36 bottom left, 38, 39 bottom, 40 bottom
left, 41, 42 right, 42 bottom left, 44, 45 top left, 46 top right, 46 bottom left, 47,
48 top right, 48 bottom left, 49, 50 top, 50 bottom, 51, 53 top, 53 bottom, 54
top, 54 bottom, 55, 56 bottom right, 57, 58 top, 60, 62 left, 62 right, 65 bottom
right, 66, 68, 69 left, 69 right, 70, 71 top left, 72 right, 72 centre, 73, 75 left,
75 right, 76, 77 left, 77 right, 78, 79 top, 80, 81 top, 81 bottom, 82, 83 left,
83 right, 84, 85, 86, 88, 89 top, 89 bottom, 90, 91 right, 91 top

Andrew Lawson 12, 39 top, 40 top right, 43

Photos Horticultural 4, 20, 29 bottom, 36 bottom right, 45 centre right, 56
top left, 58 bottom, 59 top, 61 bottom, 64, 65 top, 67 top, 92

Harry Smith Collection 17, 18, 63 right, 67 bottom, 71 bottom, 74